HISTORICAL VIGNETTES

DAVID NEWSOME

BY THE SAME AUTHOR

A History of Wellington College (1959)

Godliness and Good Learning (1961)

The Parting of Friends (1966)

Two Classes of Men (1974)

On the Edge of Paradise (1980)

Edwardian Excursions (1981)

The Convert Cardinals (1993)

The Victorian World Picture (1997)

HISTORICAL VIGNETTES

David Newsome

Edited by Serenhedd James

First published in 2011

ISBN 978-1-4709-2200-9

CONTENTS

Foreword vii

David Newsome: An Appreciation ix

Editor's Note xiii

Author's Preface xv

I. In Defence of History (1986) 1

II. Two Cambridge Historians (1966) 19

III. The Emotive Nature of Victorian Prose (1985) 35

IV. Thomas Arnold: A Bicentenary Appraisal (1995) 53

V. Newman & the Oxford Movement (1968) 75

VI. Three Brothers: A.C., E.F., & R.H. Benson (1986) 95

VII. 'How Soapy was Sam?': A Study of Samuel Wilberforce (1963) 115

VIII. 'The Assault on Mammon': Charles Gore & John Neville Figgis (1965) 131

IX. The Novels of Charles Dickens: Fact & Fiction (2001) 151

References 167

FOREWORD

When our father died in 2004, he left the manuscript for this collection of articles, with the wish that they should one day be made available to those who wished to read them. It is perhaps not inappropriate that they should see the light of day exactly 50 years after the publication of *Godliness and Good Learning,* the book that first brought him renown as a social and ecclesiastical historian of the Victorian period. None of the articles included here are readily available, and three have never previously been published at all. This collection represents the last of our father's work, and his original manuscript is reproduced with only minor editorial alterations. We would like to thank Dr Serenhedd James for editing the manuscript, as well as for his enormous support and encouragement. We are also deeply grateful to Bishop Geoffrey Rowell for writing an appreciation of our father's role as an historian to accompany these articles.

The picture we have chosen for the cover is of Christopher Wordsworth, Bishop of Lincoln, drawn by George Richmond. The original sketch hung in our father's study until his death, a gift from Dr Octavia Wilberforce with whom he worked on the Wilberforce papers for *The Parting of Friends*. He was very taken with the drawing when he first saw it and described it in his diary as 'beautiful'. On 1 March 1961, he wrote 'After lunch, as I was taking my leave, looking with envious eyes at the sketch of Christopher Wordsworth, she said, that if our partnership were productive, she would give me it – just fancy!' It became one of his most precious possessions and so seems a fitting picture to illustrate his final work. Following his death we felt it right to return it to the Wordsworth family and it now hangs in Dorothy Wordsworth's bedroom at Rydal Mount. We are grateful to Susan Andrew for allowing us to reproduce it here.

Clare, Janet, Louise & Cordelia *nées* Newsome

DAVID NEWSOME: AN APPRECIATION

The Right Reverend Dr Geoffrey Rowell: Bishop of Gibraltar in Europe and Emeritus Fellow of Keble College, Oxford

I am delighted that this collection of David Newsome's essays and papers, written and delivered over a number of years and for a number of different audiences, has been made available to a wider readership.

I first met David Newsome when he taught me for the nineteenth-century paper of the Theological Tripos at Cambridge in the early 1960s. Enthused by his supervisions and equally by his lectures – informative, amusing and instructive – I was delighted to have David as my research supervisor when I started graduate work. Originally intending to work on the history of the Anglo-Prussian bishopric in Jerusalem, hoping this would enable me to build on a developing interest in the Orthodox Churches, I changed after little more than a term to a very different topic: 'Death and the Future Life in the Religious Thought of Nineteenth-Century England.' I remember a long and helpful discussion with David in a Cambridge curry house, where we weighed the pros and cons of this change of direction. There were those, I learned later, on the research committee of the Divinity Faculty who thought my proposed new topic too wide-ranging; I am sure it was in part David's advocacy that led to the formal approval of my thesis topic.

Cambridge in the mid-sixties was blessed with three remarkable experts in nineteenth-century church history: the magisterial Owen Chadwick, who gave me a wonderful gift as a young scholar by asking me to check the references for the first volume of his *Victorian Church*; Alec Vidler, Dean of King's, sporting a white tie rather than a clerical collar, and black and white French *curé* bands when in choir dress; and David Newsome. One year I estimated there were twenty-five graduate students working on various aspects of the nineteenth-century church.

David was an enthusiast, and an historian with a deep empathy for the people whose lives and ideas he studied. Blessed with a rare felicity of style and an eye for detail, I can recall him advising me to make sure, if I came across a reference to the colour of the drawing-room curtains in original letters, that I noted it down, even if it was not what I was looking for – 'You never know when you might need it to evoke a sense of place!'

David enthused about ideas, and about people. *Two Classes of Men* explores Platonism and Aristotelianism in Victorian England. His *History of Wellington College* (which led to his moving his interests from the Middle Ages to the nineteenth century), brought school history to a new place in serious social history. *Godliness and Good Learning* explored further the Victorian educational ideal, which was to be complemented later on by his quarrying of A. C. Benson's massive diaries for *On the Edge of Paradise,* with its sensitive and sympathetic exploration of the delicate art of schoolmastering, Benson's mordant comments and acute observation as a voyeur of life, and the subtle complexities of Benson's personality. *The Parting of Friends* drew on the rich cache of Wilberforce papers to throw new light on the drama of the Oxford Movement, previously seen through the eyes of Newman's *Apologia* and Dean Church's classic history. The poignancy of the shattering of family relationships as religious paths diverged was again sensitively captured, and the underlying theological issues no less clearly explored. Henry Manning was a central character in *The Parting of Friends,* and David was always a defender of Manning's greatness against the more ardent 'Newmanistes' – a theme explored again in one of his later books, *The Convert Cardinals.* His expertise in painting on a large canvas, drawing the big picture with his *pointilliste* eye for detail and judicious use of vignette enabled him to produce *The Victorian World Picture.*

In *The Idea of a University* Newman said that a university without the influence of teachers on pupils would be 'a frozen, ice-bound, petrified university'. Newman realised that truth had to be embodied and that personal influence was the means of communicating the Gospel. David Newsome held that to be no less true of the university teacher and the schoolmaster. As one of his graduate students I owe him much beyond the imparting of academic information. A research supervisor who would regularly gather his pupils for a relaxed and enjoyable dinner was light years away from the need to clock up on some score-sheet the number of 'student contact hours'. When I myself became a research supervisor over many years in Oxford it was a great pleasure to do the same, and also to invite David from Wellington to come and join the company. These essays and papers, chosen by David himself may be a reminder of an earlier style of doing history; they are certainly a fitting memorial to a great teacher who gave much to many – not least enduring friendship and encouragement.

✠ Geoffrey Gibraltar

EDITOR'S NOTE

History can accord very few men the distinction of having been successively Scholar, Fellow and Senior Tutor of a Cambridge college, then headmaster of two of England's leading public schools, and simultaneously to have established and maintained an international reputation as a leading scholar of the religious and social history of his chosen era.

In this, his final published work, we see the strains of David Newsome's academic interests and personal passions come together as he defends the vital pursuit of historical truth, and considers some of the influences which set him on his path as one of its champions. We see his insightful treatment of some of the characters who lend to Victorian England a great deal of its fascination for the historian; always sympathetic, but never hagiographical. We also encounter the great breadth of his scholarship in his considerations of some of the literature of the period; from which, quite apart from his writing, he clearly derived a great deal of pleasure.

David Newsome was possessed of that prized skill of the historian: the ability to look at his subjects through the eyes of their contemporaries, and to talk and write about his period as if he himself had been there. He lived in the days when it was still possible for a schoolmaster to be elected to a Cambridge fellowship, and for a college fellow to be appointed to the headmastership of a school. In the mould of Dr Arnold of Rugby, he was a very great schoolmaster-scholar; perhaps, even, he was the last.

He was a man, take him for all in all,
I shall not look upon his like again.

Serenhedd James

I had a ridiculous dream last night about a meeting in the Senate House to debate the canonisation of John Henry Newman, I leading the opposition, stoutly arguing Manning's case. In the end a class list was published with Newman in the First Class and Manning getting a Third!

Extract from the diaries of David Newsome, 7 June 1963

I was so absorbed in my work this morning that I forgot my name! When I went to the parlour for coffee, I looked at the list to tick off my name and was puzzled that I could not find it. I was looking for 'Wilberforce'!

Extract from the diaries of David Newsome, 12 September 1964

AUTHOR'S PREFACE

I have entitled this collection of nine articles or lectures, written or delivered over a time span of nearly forty years, *Historical Vignettes*, because insofar as the wide range of subjects covered has a linking theme, the word 'vignette' would seem to be the most appropriate. The opening paper on the study of History, for instance, puts forward my personal conviction that the historian's first duty is to attempt to recreate a vivid and faithful picture of the past, and of the flesh and blood of past ages, through a 'mosaic of vignette-studies'. The final paper on the novels of Dickens suggests that their chief value to the historian lies in their graphic vignettes of early nineteenth-century and mid-Victorian life, unrecoverable from other sources. Most of the intervening papers are primarily biographical vignettes – character studies in which chosen subjects are depicted in such a way as to render them (and their different viewpoints and stances) not only credible to a later age, but also as living people for whom one can feel a certain degree of empathy.

The prose writers of the Victorian age understood the importance of securing their readers' empathy for whatever their subject matter might be and unashamedly strove to appeal to the heart as much as to the head. For this reason I have included a lecture I gave to the Royal Society of Literature in which I illustrated some of the techniques that they were wont to employ. On a personal note, when I came to sort through past lectures and articles, some unpublished, others that appeared in periodicals not now easily available, I found that I was selecting those which, at the time, gave me most enjoyment in writing. I therefore hope that something of that enjoyment will be shared by my readers.

David Newsome

I am grateful to Emmanuel College, The Royal Society of Literature, SPCK, *History Today* and Cambridge University Press respectively, for permission to reprint articles II, III, V, VII and VIII. Full details of their first appearance can be found on the title page for each article.

I

IN DEFENCE OF HISTORY

In November 1986, the Rev'd Gordon Wakefield of Queen's College, Birmingham, organised an interdenominational conference for students of theological colleges and seminaries in the Midlands area, inviting various speakers to talk about their particular field of study with a view to exhibiting not only its importance as a discipline for serious research but also as having significant interest for the non-specialist. My particular brief was to state the case for the defence of the study of History.

In publishing this paper many years after it was delivered, I am conscious that the focus of historical study has been gradually but perceptibly shifting away from the exclusively classical and Christian traditions of Western Europe in which I was nurtured in the Cambridge of the early 1950s, and that with that shift have come certain new and more technical approaches to methodology. Nevertheless, since a defence of the discipline that has been the enduring fascination of my professional life must, it seems to me, be based on one's personal experience and particular interests, I am happy that it should stand exactly as it was originally delivered.

I

IN DEFENCE OF HISTORY

Queen's College, Birmingham, 16 November 1986

Let me begin with a television commercial, possibly imperfectly remembered, as television commercials tend to be. What was being advertised, as I recall, was a brand of jeans worn by a sinuous youth who, as he modelled the product in question, sang a rather catchy song, which – I am told – was sufficiently popular to score high ratings in the charts. The melody escapes me, as do most of the words, apart from the opening line of the lyric which went as follows: 'I don't know much history', and culminated in the punch-line 'but I'm having a wonderful time'. As the song developed, the youth admitted to indifference to various other disciplines as well, but it was the original disclaimer that has stuck in my mind, together with the very questionable conclusion that ignorance of history ministers to a happy and carefree life. Not only do I believe this to be untrue, but I should go so far as to say that it is the very reverse of truth. Yet the sentiment, expressed in a less naïve and less colourful way, is sometimes encountered among the young today, brought up as they are in the age of high technology and looking, perhaps, to a future that has quite self-consciously freed itself from the shackles of the past. They want to build a new and better world, rather than to be reminded of the manifest failures of their forefathers. What is past is past: if it is the property of old men to dream dreams, then it is the prerogative of youth to see visions, for they are tomorrow's people.

'Tomorrow's people' has a grand and rather optimistic ring about it. Indeed, I have heard the phrase used eloquently by preachers in addresses of urgent idealism to a congregation of teenage boys and girls. The phrase, however, means nothing if 'tomorrow's people' do not at the same time acknowledge that they are also 'yesterday's heirs'. Whether they like it or not, they are what history has made them. Even their very distrust of history has been shaped by history itself. The prejudices, for instance, which cause them to accept uncritically one set of values and to dismiss contemptuously another are the products of the past. Similarly, both national and denominational alienation can have roots so deep that only an understanding of history can expose inherited prejudices for what they truly are: the hatred in times past of Athens for Sparta or the instinctive revulsion by a Jew for a Samaritan; in more recent times, the distrust of Frenchmen for Germans; and very much nearer to home, the hostility of the Arab world towards the Israelis and the seemingly irreconcilable enmity between Catholics and Protestants, or more accurately Nationalists and Loyalists, in Ireland.

If history has created such divisions, it might be said that it were better for history to be forgotten. It is not, however, as simple as that. The inherited prejudices remain and can only be conquered if faced up to and understood. History cannot be unmade, nor can we escape from it. A young German may prefer not to know what the Nazis did to Jews in extermination camps like Auschwitz and Treblinka, but he ignores it at his peril. As G. M. Young once observed: if you try to escape from your history, you lose interest in yourself. That way, civilisations have died: 'They perished because they lost interest in themselves.'

'Know thyself' is one of the oldest and wisest precepts that have come to us from the ancient world. Knowing yourself in order to discover the prejudices that you have inherited, or the crimes that your ancestors have committed, may seem something of a negative exercise, but there is a positive side. This is how the historian-philosopher, R. G. Collingwood, once expressed it:

> History is 'for' human self-knowledge. It is generally thought to be of importance to man that he should know himself; where knowing himself means not his merely personal peculiarities, the things that distinguish him from other men, but his nature as man. Knowing

> yourself means knowing, first, what it is to be a man; secondly; knowing what it is to be the kind of man you are and nobody else is. Knowing yourself means knowing what you can do; and since nobody knows what he can do until he tries, the only clue to what man can do is what man has done. The value of history, then, is that it teaches us what man has done and thus what man is.

So much to the point is this that I am tempted to say that my case rests there. Some examples, however, both hypothetical and concrete, may serve as necessary elaboration.

Let us suppose, for one moment, that we could obliterate the past. Let us say that some appalling cataclysm has overcome the civilised world so that civilisation as we know it has been wiped out. There would, we might suppose, be little pockets of survivors, hanging on to life and then trying to form some basic social community in which some semblance of civilisation could be rebuilt. This is a favourite *mis-en-scene*, of course, of science fiction. In order to survive, you would need some good men and true to find food and then to grow food in order to perpetuate the supply of the necessities of life. The building of this new world would call for manual skills first of all; and then, if you were able to survive this rudimentary stage, the next need would be for technologists, scientists, doctors and engineers. Of what use would the historian be then? It would depend, doubtless, on what sort of civilisation you were trying to rebuild. Man cannot, and never could, live upon bread alone, and there would be, I suspect, a desperate craving for some intellectual and cultural tradition. A skeleton library, could it have survived the holocaust, would be a boon beyond price, especially if it contained the corpus of past knowledge in which future scientists and technologists could be trained. What else? A Bible, a Shakespeare, perhaps; and other literary monuments, too, if one wanted to recover the genius of civilisation of the Western world.

In his Foundation Oration at Birkbeck College, London, in 1946 G. M. Young (to whom I unashamedly turn for a second time) had this to say on just such a theme: 'If ever the Dark Ages return', he wrote, 'and two such books only come through, then, if those books were Aristotle's *Ethics* and Newman's *Idea of a University*, they would be enough to show a reviving world what civilisation meant.' Such a choice might seem to an audience such as this rather too obviously a historian's quirk or predilection. Here might be, you may feel, a God-sent opportunity to bury the conceits of a past that had come so devastatingly to grief, and to try to create some entirely new intellectual and cultural tradition. How far would you get, I wonder, without reliance upon the past?

In his novel of survival, *The Day of the Triffids*, John Wyndham poses the same question and answers it through the mouth of the self-appointed leader of one of the groups of survivors, Coker:

> From my reading of history the thing you have to have to use knowledge is leisure ... The thinking has to be done largely by people who are not directly productive ... Learning grew up in the cities and in great institutions. It was the labour of the countryside that supported them ... To hold us over, to make any use at all of the knowledge in the libraries we must have the teachers, the doctors and the leaders, and we must be able to support them while they help us.

This, in itself, is an historical judgment, based on the knowledge of how learning advanced. Later on, in the same book, when the two main characters, Stephen and Josella, are discussing how they will explain their new world to their children, they come to the conclusion that they have to be able to present a story of their past. If they have no past, they will have no inspiration. If the past leading up to the catastrophe itself is too grim to pass on to posterity, then they will have to create a myth instead. Only then, says Josella, will they find 'the incentive to build' and 'this time to build something better'. Plato had said something similar two thousand years earlier in *The Republic.* The few – the *cognoscenti*

– must know the truth about their origins. For the many who could not understand it, a 'noble lie' (or an approximation to the truth expressed in allegorical terms) must be invented in order to satisfy man's need for an explanation of the natural ordering of society.

A red light for danger flickers here. Respect for history can sometimes be a cloak for disrespect; its use can easily conceal sinister abuse. To invent history, or rather to distort it for political ends and for the sake of propaganda (not unknown in recent times within totalitarian regimes) is a crime against truth itself. A historian may err unwittingly because of the very subjective nature of the interpretation of evidence. But deliberately to pass off legend as truth for nationalistic purposes is to deepen the very inherited prejudices which a dispassionate study of the past might have been able to cure. The greatest service that the professional study of history can render is to train minds to be able to discover the deliberate falsification of facts, and thereby to expose propaganda for what it is.

To try to recover the past in order to learn from both its insights and its mistakes is, however, another matter altogether. How, in actual historical fact, have civilisations weathered the storm of collapse and disintegration? The Roman Empire took an unconscionable time a-dying; and its death agonies in the fourth and fifth centuries were both conspicuously terminal and psychologically demoralising for those who witnessed the slow destruction by the barbarian marauders of almost everything that had ministered to the splendour and the glory that had once been Rome's. Order, administration, culture, commerce and technology crumpled under the strain and devastation of war, vandalism, insecurity and plague. Nevertheless, in those times of horror, the Christian Church came to the rescue, providing the vestiges of order in times of disorder, and small oases of tranquillity and peace in the form of the Benedictine religious houses, safeguarding something of the literary treasures of both the Christian and the pagan past. What Western culture and civilisation have owed to monasticism is incalculable, both in the dark times of the disintegrating Empire and in later ages too. After the collapse of the first, highly precarious, experiment in Europeanism, if as such one can describe the Empire of Charlemagne, again the labours of monks and scholars at the palace school at Aachen preserved from the past those seminal texts, copied in meticulous miniscule, which would form the basis of that revival of learning in the twelfth century deservedly acquiring the description of 'Renaissance'.

The past, again, provided the inspiration. 'In antiquis est scientia' was the slogan of the twelfth-century scholars as it was, at least implicitly, of the humanists of the Italian Renaissance (and of the Renaissance in Northern Europe at the close of the fifteenth century). The rebuilding of the new world was founded upon, and inspired by, the genius of the old; and therefore the primary task of these medieval and Renaissance scholars was to delve into history to recover the *Corpus Juris Civilis* (if they were lawyers), the patristic writings and, later, the original Gospel texts (if they were theologians); and for the benefit of all of them, the polymathic Aristotelian treatises on philosophy, politics, ethics, and science, giving way in time to the newly-translated *Dialogues* of Plato, as the schoolmen gave way to the humanists.

Quite explicitly, they were saying: where would civilisation be without the lessons, the wisdom and the genius of the past? This does not mean that they were slavishly imitative or that they were inhibited from acknowledging the creative insights of their own generation. The stance that they took was expressed memorably by the twelfth-century scholar, Bernard of Chartres:

> We are as dwarves mounted on the shoulders of giants, so that we can see more and further than they; yet not by virtue of the keenness of our eyesight; nor through the tallness of our stature, but because we are raised and borne aloft upon that giant mass.

I believe, as an historian, that this is a timeless truth; an image for all times. Whatever our conceits may be in an age that accepts progress as a norm, and tends to equate progress with advanced technology and increasing material prosperity, we are more dependent than we are inclined to acknowledge on the wisdom and perceptions of the past; and this surely is one of the duties of the historian to discover and to pass on to his own generation.

Fully to appreciate this, we have to be able to recognise the highly significant distinction between knowledge and wisdom. To know is one thing; to understand, another. No one can doubt that the quest for knowledge is innate in man. We are naturally curious creatures. You have only to look at a young child to see the proof of this. He is forever asking questions, and usually posing the question – 'why?' (a question, one might observe, that as often as not requires an historical answer because it is the most frequent one that an historian poses himself). Furthermore, no one would dispute the fact that the advance in sheer knowledge over the last two centuries, especially in terms of science and technology, in satisfying our desire to know how the universe works and how its workings can be exploited to our ends, has been so rapid that it must pass the comprehension and wildest imaginings of our forefathers two hundred years ago.

C. S. Lewis argued, in his Inaugural Lecture at Cambridge as Professor of Medieval and Renaissance Studies, that one of the reasons why we must regard modernity as something much more recent than the traditional ending of the Middle Ages at the close of the fifteenth century, was that 'between [the age of] Jane Austen and us, but not between her and Shakespeare, Chaucer, Alfred, Virgil, Homer, and the Pharaohs, comes the birth of the machines'. It can be seen most obviously in the changed meanings of certain words:

> How has it come about that we use the highly emotive word 'stagnation' with all its malodorous and malarial overtones, for

> what other ages would have called 'permanence'? Why does the word 'primitive' at once suggest to us clumsiness, inefficiency, barbarity? When our ancestors talked of the primitive church or the primitive purity of our constitution they meant nothing of that sort. (The only pejorative sense which Johnson gives to primitive in his Dictionary is, significantly, 'Formal; affectedly solemn; imitating the supposed gravity of old times'.) Why does 'latest' in advertisements mean 'best'?

The answer is obvious: 'In the world of machines, the new most often really is better and the primitive really is clumsy.' The consequence, however, of this quite understandable scale of values is that it so elevates the superiority of knowledge, which is seen everywhere to advance, that the insights of former ages that lived in ignorance of our scientific and technological discoveries can only too easily be dismissed with swift contempt.

Again, we may turn to John Wyndham for a timely word of caution. In another of his novels, *The Midwich Cuckoos,* Wyndham's essentially Platonic approach to the problems of the modern world is articulated by the character, Zellaby. 'None of this knowledge', Zellaby says, 'is of the least use until it is informed by understanding. Knowledge is simply a kind of fuel which needs the motor of understanding to convert it into power'. He is in fact echoing the words of the writer of the *Proverbs*, while changing the metaphor for the sake of a modern audience: 'Through wisdom is an house builded, and by understanding it is established. By knowledge are the chambers filled.'

In the ancient world, as in the early Middle Ages, wisdom was considered to be the prerogative of age. If one applies this principle to the time-scale of the development of the Western world, there is a certain irony in seeking wisdom from an era when the world was comparatively young. Yet there is some truth in it. It is as if the very acceleration of scientific and technological knowledge in the last two hundred years has somehow outpaced the ability to comprehend it in the way which understanding or wisdom require. Whatever wisdom may be, it is the capacity to view the parts as a whole; to observe what was and what is now *sub specie æternitatis*; to see the interrelation of all things within the context of abiding and timeless truths. It may not be within the faculties of man to aspire to such a vision, because if one takes the Latin maxim literally there is no man so polymathic, and never has been, that he can claim for himself the vantage-point of the Creator alone. But if there is any discipline whose practitioners are capable of taking 'upon's the mystery of things as if we were God's spies', then I believe that History may most nearly make that claim.

These things are more easily said than exemplified, of course. I can offer one personal reflection. It was actually a German physicist and philosopher, Leibnitz, who first enunciated one of the most penetrating observations about the process of dialectic which can be traced in history even over a relatively narrow time-span, 'Do not despise anything', he wrote, because 'men are usually right in what they affirm and wrong in what they deny.' This dictum was eagerly seized upon by Coleridge as yet another confirmation of what he believed to be a universal law: that the essence of truth lies in the phrase 'coincidentia oppositorum', or the reconciliation of opposites. The student of ecclesiastical history may well come to the same conclusion, surveying as he is bound to do the frequency with which a truth proclaimed and cherished by one particular prophet in his generation is so swiftly pushed to extremes that it becomes a half-truth, requiring the corrective of reaction to redress the balance. From his own researches he will be inclined to acknowledge that man's apprehension of truth is almost always too narrow. Whatever truth may be, it is rarely 'Either-Or', but more usually 'Both-And'.

This, as I have said, is a personal conviction from my own study of history, and I do not suggest that it will be acceptable to all. Nor, in making such a sweeping statement am I trying to supply an apologia for what may be called 'broad-brush' history, from which I have never personally derived much inspiration or instruction. The truths that history teaches can be discerned more clearly, I believe, rather on the small canvas than the large. The insights of the historian come from the mosaic of vignette-studies by devoted historical scholars who absorb themselves totally into the minutiæ and mores of the problem or period they may be studying. Whether it be the detailed evocation of the life of a cathedral city (Angers) in early eighteenth-century France, from the pen of John MacManners, or the analysis in depth of the meaning of the single word 'Buzones' in a medieval law-book by G. T. Lapsley, something living from the past is made to live again; and our understanding of man and society is thereby enriched.

We enter here into the arena of current controversy, best expressed by the question 'Has not overmuch study of the tiny parts obscured rather than clarified our understanding of the whole?' In an article in *The Times Literary Supplement*, David Cannadine has argued that such an approach has all but killed respect for history amongst laymen. The study of history has turned, in the hands of professionalism, into such an obsessive preoccupation with minutiæ that the result has been to engender a combination of 'intellectual timidity and antiquarian pedantry'. History, he argues, has become at one and the same time too scholarly and too critical, shying away from good healthy controversy and provocative generalisation. The end result of being 'more concerned with trivial truth than with fertile error' has been to make of the discipline 'little more than an intellectual pastime for consenting adults in private'.

Now these warnings have been issued before and in much the same language. Some years before in his Inaugural Lecture at Oxford, Hugh Trevor-Roper declared that 'History that is not useful, that has not some lay appeal is mere antiquarianism; history that is not controversial is dead history, and neither dead history nor antiquarianism deserve a regius chair'. Herein, he argues, lies the major distinction between history, as one of the humane studies, and the exact sciences.

> The fact that a branch of physics or mathematics may be quite beyond the interest or comprehension of an educated layman in no way invalidates it, because the validity of such subjects do not depend on lay comprehension ... But the humane studies are quite different from this. They have no direct scientific use; ... they exist primarily not for the training of professionals, but for the education of laymen; and therefore if they once lose touch with the lay mind, they are rightly condemned to perish.

In a passage which David Cannadine must have unconsciously called to mind when writing his own article, Trevor-Roper concludes: 'In humane studies there are times when a new error is more life-giving than an old truth, a fertile error than a sterile accuracy.' I should certainly concede that the study of history would have been the poorer without, for instance, Henri Pirenne's controversial thesis on Mohammed and Charlemagne, when he described the Mediterranean as a Moslem lake, or Max Weber's celebrated linking of capitalism with the Protestant ethic. They duly provoked stimulating debate and productive research either to substantiate or to refute the theories that had been advanced.

In the face of this strong fighting talk, my defence of history as a mosaic of vignette-studies would seem to be somewhat shaken. Yet I can accept the main thrust of what these two scholars have written without shifting my ground. Trevor-Roper is at pains to point out that it is not research that he is attacking, but rather something called 'professionalism'. David Cannadine is not scoffing at PhDs but the 'PhD mentality'. History would, of course become totally stagnant without research; and the whole of history can never be more than the sum of its parts. Here we may gain some guidance from Sir Isaiah

Berlin who, in his celebrated study of Tolstoy's approach to history, entitled *The Hedgehog and the Fox*, suggests that all thinkers and historians tend to fall into one of two categories, the idea originating from a fragment of an obscure Greek poet (Archilochus), transcribed as follows: 'the fox knows many things, but the hedgehog knows one big thing'. The fox is devious enough to have learnt many arts; but the hedgehog, with the one big thing he knows (or his over-view, if we put it another way), outwits him in the end.

Of course, we may interpret this as we will. Berlin, however, represents Tolstoy as a thinker who was a fox by nature wanting to be a hedgehog. Expressed in more conventional terms, Tolstoy's approach to history was initially inductive and empiricist, supposing that if one could collate all the observable facts about mankind, the mystery of man and his destiny would be a mystery no more. But both Hegel, with his over-view of history as following the law of dialectical progression, and after him Karl Marx, fascinated Tolstoy until, from his own experience, he came to the reluctant conclusion that much of what Hegel wrote was metaphysical gibberish. Having disposed of Hegel's 'big idea', however, he failed to supply a satisfactory one of his own.

Tolstoy was actually a more skilful fox than he gave himself credit for. Turgenov had pressed him to appreciate the value of recalling vignettes from the past by steeping himself in the actual lives of the men he was describing – 'their thoughts, knowledge, poetry, music, love, friendship, hates, passions' – because from these things 'real life was compounded'. And Tolstoy succeeded wonderfully in doing exactly that in *War and Peace*. But still he was not satisfied, regarding these evocations of the past as mere 'trivial flowers' rather than the roots which the over-view or the 'big idea' could discern.

This has a certain relevance to the nature of historical research as it has proliferated in recent years. A great deal, more perhaps than we suppose, follows the method of the fox. That great master-mind of the ancient world, Aristotle, wished to discover if a study of existing constitution would reveal some general laws about the origins, purposes, and stability of political communities. He therefore set his pupils at the Lyceum the task of studying, in manageable quotas, all the 158 constitutions then available for effective research. From their collective theses he compiled one of the greatest treatises on the nature of Politics that the world has ever seen. Such an exercise of directed research is commonplace in the experimental and exact sciences. One caveat, however, should be borne in mind when the same process is applied to historical research. Some years ago, the German medievalist, Ernst Bernheim, convinced that the writings of St Augustine and the world-view contained therein dominated the thought of Western Christendom up to and including the twelfth century, set several of his students to prepare doctoral theses on individual medieval thinkers with the express intention of extracting examples of Augustinian influence. Few would question Bernheim's over-view of early medieval thought; but the methodology is not without its perils. If the 'big idea' comes first and research is directed to confirm a conclusion already arrived at, the danger is that the researcher will discover what he had been told to seek and ignore everything else. In this way, the fox is really the hedgehog in disguise.

It is easy to mock the seemingly grotesque erudition or parochialism of doctoral theses. My experience is that they are rarely as trivial as their titles sometimes suggest. David Cannadine reminds us of that pathetic work of pseudo-scholarship written by the eponymous hero of Kingsley Amis's *Lucky Jim*, entitled *The Economic Influences of the Development of Shipbuilding Techniques 1450-1485*. This is caricature of course; but actually, as Professor Geoffrey Best has pointed out, the subject is by no means as ridiculous as it sounds. If it could be profitably researched, it would probably turn out to be of considerable significance to our understanding of the late fifteenth century. The writing of so-called 'tunnel history' (an expression coined by Professor J. H. Hexter) is often less of an indictment of the subject studied than of the way in which it is studied. Parochial subjects do not necessarily denote a parochial mind. 'There is really nothing wrong in thinking in tunnels', Geoffrey Elton once wrote, 'provided one remembers that there is earth above and around the tunnel, and that the shape and direction of the tunnel are governed by the constitution of the substance above it'.

The critics may still be sharpening their knives, however. *Lucky Jim*'s un-momentous offering to historical scholarship might tell us something of significance about the fifteenth century, but what conceivable relevance could it have for us today? That is not a question, however, which historians are wont to pose. They study a problem; a person; a period; in order to illuminate the past, not the present. It may be that in the course of doing so they enhance our understanding of the present, but this should never be their primary objective. Indeed, in order to understand the past, they must do their utmost to obliterate all thoughts about the present. They have to shed their contemporary outlook in order to immerse themselves in a relatively alien world. As L. P. Hartley expressed it so memorably in the opening sequence of his novel, *The Go-Between*, 'The past is a foreign country; they do things differently there.'

Unless one is prepared to recognise this, the customary will appear quaint, the very landscape will become distorted, reactions and responses will be misunderstood. Only when the study has been completed may significant consequences occur or fascinating, if sometimes perilous, affinities emerge. This is why history is often a doubtful guide to political action and should only be regarded as such with the utmost caution. It would probably be as rash a historical judgment to say that history never repeats itself as to postulate that it sometimes does. But when a parallel situation appears to arise, which forces one to recall events of the past, very rarely can one be confident that the circumstances are exactly the same. General historical propositions, drawn from sufficient evidence to promote lively and productive discussion, are, of course, an entirely different matter. Lord Acton's famous dictum, in a letter to Mandell Creighton, that 'power tends to corrupt and absolute power corrupts absolutely', and statements such as 'persecution never succeeds' or, 'woe to thee, O land, when thy king is a child', may not be universal truths, but they have enough substance in them to warrant serious reflection.

The study of history, as has been said, cannot be an exact science, and for many reasons. The quest for the truth can rarely be totally objective; and although contemporary revisionists may sometimes delude themselves into supposing that they have said the final word on a particular subject, they surely know in their heart of hearts that their conclusions can never really be definitive. This is because an historian can never be sure that he has studied all the available evidence, or – if he is really honest with himself – that he has always been scrupulously detached in the evaluation of the evidence that he has used. Then again, as G. M. Trevelyan once observed, in his essay on *Clio: A Muse*, while walking one day along the sides of Great Gable in the Lake District, he was puzzled by the fact that Helvellyn looked a totally different mountain from a vantage-point that was new to him. At first he failed to recognise it for what it was. This can sometimes be true of historical study when some particular problem of the past is viewed from a new angle or standpoint.

So it is that one of the most fascinating aspects of the study of history is that it can never really end. We have become more sophisticated in our techniques for unearthing the truth about the past since an anonymous monk of Whitby compiled the first recorded life of Pope Gregory the Great at some date between 704 and 714. But we can still learn from his disarming confession of the inadequacies of his work. He exhorts his readers 'not to nibble with critical teeth at this work of ours which has been diligently twisted into shape by love rather than knowledge ... Because we must always strive for universal truth, we have told the truth so far as in us lies'.

'The truth so far as in us lies' – has there ever been a better description of what the objective of an historian should be? I hope that this will cast some illumination on why history, of all the humane studies, is both the most compelling and the most instructive. It is hard to put into words what lies behind that compulsion to search for more and more enlightenment about the distant past, and an historian may not give any conscious thought to why he chooses this discipline as the occupation of his life; it may be just a sort of empathy with a time gone by that he finds irresistible. If he seeks to justify his work, that will come later, because he has never really sought to justify his labours to himself. The nearest I can come to expressing this is to conclude with a passage from Sir Maurice Powicke's essay on 'Historical Study in Oxford', where he is trying to explain why he fell in love with the Middle Ages.

> Shepherds have kept their sheep in all ages; why am I stirred so deeply because I can trace the very sheepwalks of the monks of Furness? Why is there a remote, yet strangely familiar music about the names of places – Beverley, Gainsborough, Thrapston, Tewkesbury – a music in which it is impossible to distinguish the call of authentic English speech from the echoes of a hundred different associations? This is more than the obstinate survival of the splendid, if ignorant, excitement of the Romantic movement ... It is the sense of the past which comes to us from the Middle Ages as it came to the young American in Henry James' story, as he wandered about his eighteenth-century house in London – the sense of a 'conscious past, recognising no less than recognisable'. The place was a museum, 'but a museum of held reverberations'. So long as we are conscious of these 'held reverberations', history will continue to entice us. So long as their mystery endures, and it will always endure, the past will continue to escape us.

II

TWO CAMBRIDGE HISTORIANS

This article first appeared in the *Emmanuel College Magazine* for the years 1965-1966, and was later reprinted in the Centenary edition of the Magazine. It commemorates two figures who, until their deaths in the same year, had dominated the teaching of History in the College since the First World War. It is difficult to imagine any two men, working for so long together in partnership, to have been so totally different in personality and in their respective approaches to the study and teaching of history. This article also recalls a chapter of University history when dons could, if they wished, devote practically the whole of their working lives to the instruction of undergraduates without any sense of compulsion to 'publish or perish'. One of the very few things that these two historians had in common was that they wrote very little but taught much.

II

TWO CAMBRIDGE HISTORIANS

Edward Welbourne and Bertram Goulding Brown enjoyed a teaching partnership, preparing Emmanuel men for the History Tripos, for close on fifty years. I have yet to meet an Emmanuel historian of senior standing who was not taught by one or other of them, or (as was more usual) both. And since the experience was unforgettable, the meeting of one's own kind over the years would lead, as a matter of course, to the exchange of 'Welbournisms' and common reminiscences of 'B.G.B.' muffling himself up against the cold or expounding Stubbs' *Select Charters* in high and querulous tones. What Tait and Tout had been to Manchester, these two were to us: great originals, men who in our imagination could never have been pupils; teachers who never ceased to teach. Their pupils came back when they could, and whatever distinctions they might have acquired in the intervening years counted for nothing from the very moment of confrontation: the old relationship was at once resumed. One hesitated to advance an opinion lest it should be shattered by a Welbournian paradox. One stammered incoherently to Goulding Brown for fear of wounding him with a split infinitive or souring one's good relationship with a solecism.

Those who were denied the privilege of being taught by them can never fully understand. Goulding Brown and Welbourne were almost unknown as historians to the outside world, perhaps even imperfectly appreciated in the Cambridge that was not Emmanuel College. In interpreting them to a wider public, I have to confess that I knew them only in their later years, although I suspect that their approach to history and their methods of teaching had changed very little over the decades. To enter Goulding Brown's rooms as a freshman (it was normally his task to prepare the innocents for the slaughter) was to imbibe at once the ethos of *semper eadem.* Neither furniture nor furnishings had changed since he first took root there during the 1914-18 war. Perhaps the vast library had increased (I have since discovered that most of it consisted of duplicates from the vaster library at 16, Brookside), but the piles of learned journals kept on the centre table looked so solid and undisturbed that one imagined that, could they have been moved, the surface beneath would have been found bleached and withered like grass flattened by a heavy stone. There were cabinets of various sizes, containing faded letters and spidery notes; old pipes reposing in sombre ashtrays; a mantelpiece cluttered with Christmas cards from ten years back; by the fire, two chairs: one high-backed and ample, from which the frail Edwardian figure, with long thin legs crossed above the knee and at the ankles, surveyed you solemnly as you fumbled for your essay, the other – reserved for pupils – a huge wicker monstrosity, its seat only inches from the floor, so that the act of sitting seemed like dropping into a void.

All these things are remembered by former pupils; so also the course of study which was as predictable as it was (for the middle years of the twentieth century) undoubtedly unique. One's first essay was entitled 'The Historian's Materials', and the prescribed reading began with Frederic Harrison's *The Meaning of History*, especially the first lecture originally delivered in 1862. All the subsequent essay titles conformed to a rigid pattern. The reading was meticulously devised, with exact page references, and if one was permitted to read more than was given, one most assuredly was forbidden to read less. The main fare consisted of portions of the great historical classics and the works of the titanic pioneers. On the English Manor, we read Seebohm, Maitland, and Vinogradoff; on the fall of the Roman Empire, Gibbon, Samuel Dill, and Seeley's *Lectures and Addresses*; on the barbarians, Thomas Hodgkin; on the papacy, Dean Milman and Bishop Creighton.

The larger reading-lists came in the second year. The names of Mommsen, Warde-Fowler, Zimmern, Heitland, and T. R. Glover stand out from the Ancient History list (also Sir John Mahaffy, from whose works Goulding Brown would give occasional short readings, chuckling with delight at the 'daring' prose). Freeman, Stubbs and Round were set in abundance for the English Medieval period, to supplement the long set passages from F.W. Maitland. *Domesday Book and Beyond* and S. R. Maitland's *The Dark Ages* were two of his favourite historical works. He had a high regard for Sir Frank Stenton, but little time for other moderns. Gaillard Lapsley he thought 'ingenious'.

The choice of reading dated the man, and enhanced the physical impression of immense old age. I suspect, from noting the same venerable look in a photograph of him at the chessboard with a group of Trinity undergraduates in 1902, that he was always thought to be older than he was. But his memory went back a long way. He could recall Lord Acton's rooms in Trinity; he had been taught palaeography as a B.A. by F. W. Maitland (who died in 1906); he was one of the first undergraduates to be examined under the new Historical Tripos regulations of 1901, being placed in the First Class in successive years (1902 and 1903) by examiners such as Westlake, Oscar Browning, H. A. L. Fisher and Stanley Leathes. Sir John Clapham, D. A. Winstanley, Temperley, Gooch, and Trevelyan were his immediate seniors.

To him this was the golden age of Cambridge history. He had come to Trinity from Westminster, where he had studied in the Classical VIth, and had undergone a training second to none. It was his duty to pass on what he had gained there from to a younger generation. Confronted with a young man, fresh from a specialist history sixth, thinking that he knew all the answers because he had read some selected articles in the *English Historical Review* and a bundle of Historical Association pamphlets, Goulding Brown would brush all these claims aside with bland indifference and set him going on the established routine: 'For your first essay, Frederic Harrison...'. You must have learned to walk before you could run. New ideas could be assimilated from lectures, which he regarded as compulsory, but the grounding, the method, the art of exposition were to be learned from the giants of the past.

He was right, of course. As a training both for the historian of the future and for those who were reading history to broaden their minds, the course was incomparable. He drove home one of the most important, yet neglected, truths of historical study, that the latest view is not necessarily the best; and from the experience gained from watching J. H. Round trouncing Freeman and Hubert Hall, only to be castigated (very reluctantly and very gently) by F. W. Maitland, we learnt how arrogant dogmatism in scholarship is always uncalled for and usually provokes a dreadful Nemesis. If we sometimes felt uneasy, it was because the routine never changed. We were reading what our fathers had read. I can recall starting work on a book by G. B. Grundy in the Seeley library and turning the pages which Goulding Brown had set (disconcertingly well thumbed), and finding written in the margins: 'so you too are taught by B.G.B., February 1929'.

By contrast, Welbourne was entirely unpredictable. With Goulding Brown a supervision lasted fifty minutes and not a minute more. If an essay exceeded the desired length it was stopped in mid-flow so that the necessary comments could be made. Welbourne, however, continued a supervision until his next engagement. I normally went to him at 4 p.m. on Fridays, when he offered me tea, and the supervision lasted until Hall at seven-thirty. He never set an essay title. 'Bring me another', he would say at the close of each supervision. 'Read away!' would be the first words one heard on entering his room the following week. In fact, I succeeded in reading an essay to him only once, and on that occasion he fell asleep. It was normally sufficient to read just the first sentence to let loose the stream of paradox which flowed on undisturbed, except when he paused to munch moodily at a Marie biscuit. 'Ah well', he would say, before flinging himself into some bewildering *non-sequitur*, which somehow, through devious routes, brought him back to the main track. It was always brilliant, but frequently baffling, especially since he had a habit of punctuating his observations with the remark: 'If you say that in Tripos, they'll plough you.' Looking at some notes which I attempted to take after one supervision (ostensibly on the Counter-Reformation), I find that we covered *inter alia* the childhood of Ribbentrop, the *real* story behind the building of the American railways, why London footmen were usually Irish, the origin of Lyons Corner Houses, Luther's consumption of liver-sausage and the religious significance of porridge. Somehow it all got back to the Council of Trent.

Welbourne never gave a book list. He would mention odd books in passing, and his choice was deliciously idiosyncratic – a law textbook by C. S. Fifoot, B. L. Manning's *Protestant Dissenting Deputies* (an excellent book, but the only one I can recall as recommended for modern constitutional history). He once passed me a *History of the Sulphuric Acid Industry in Cheshire* with the words: 'If you want a First in Tripos, you'd better read this. It's all in here.'

The differences between Welbourne and Goulding Brown in their approach to historical study were – it seemed to a pupil at first overwhelmed by the transition – quite fundamental. Goulding Brown had his idols and made no secret of his veneration of them. Welbourne was by nature iconoclastic and loved to unravel the machinations behind the scenes, to expose the feet of clay. Goulding Brown was very frank about his prejudices and declared them from the start. 'I am a Tory and a High Churchman', he would announce in the course of his first supervision and we were to bear that fact in mind and to assess every judgment that he vouchsafed in the light of his peculiar predilections. Not so with Welbourne. While never disguising his prejudices, he gave vent to them with such vehemence in his emphasis on the conspiratorial element in history, that he left his pupils, as often as not, with the impression that he who would slake his thirst at the fountain of history must imbibe a witches' brew, compounded of the venom of sinister papists, court toadies, pretentious *arrivistes*, hot-headed Welshmen and power-hungry Jews. There is more to history than this, and Welbourne knew it in his heart, but he did not always choose to say so.

He could be mischievous; he could be perverse; he was certainly wonderfully stimulating. 'Didn't you know *that*?' he would say, his whole body heaving with delight, after a particular outrageous *exposé*. 'It's true, isn't it?' Not many dared to challenge him, and those that did were usually worsted. He reached his position of authority through voracious reading. His method, as one would expect, was unusual. I have heard it said that he read a book a day and two on Sundays. He skipped and 'gutted' as his fancy moved him. His discerning eye picked out the relevant fact, the injudicious slip which supplied the clue to all – a clue which would have eluded ninety-nine out of a hundred readers. And the information would be docketed away in his mind. He ranged far and wide in his reading. One week he would collect a 'bag of books' (a favourite phrase) on the lesser councils of the Church, the next he would be studying the processes of glass-blowing; he would then turn to some dozen different volumes of reminiscences of the Peninsular War. It seemed to be without order or logic, the connecting links as tenuous and obscure as the sequence of his conversation. But he had read many of the books which the specialist had read, and sometimes a few which they had not, and he could take on all-comers. Even when you were fighting from a seemingly impregnable position, he somehow managed to undermine your confidence. He had spotted something which you had overlooked or perceived some subtle significance in an episode which you had discounted. I recall the tail-end of a conversation between Welbourne and a research student at a sherry party. The young man was looking flustered and indignant, but as Welbourne moved away to speak to a neighbour, he managed to blurt out a rejoinder – 'What about the Bishop of Birmingham?' Welbourne turned and chuckled: 'Yes – but who *appointed* the Bishop of Birmingham?'

Knowledge of the recondite, and the ability to employ it in argument, made Welbourne a formidable controversialist. These gifts were, however, also his bane. He could range widely, but lacked therefore the time, and perhaps the stamina, to dig down to the roots. After his research for the Prince Consort Essay (*The Miners' Unions of Northumberland and Durham*), he worked very little on original sources, and he sometimes betrayed his awareness of this Achilles heel. On one occasion, when he had finished cutting a Professor of History down to size, the affronted dignitary succeeded in wounding him with a calculated *riposte*: 'I have been working in the Public Records Office, Welbourne', he said. 'Do you know where that is?' Then again, Welbourne's knowledge was so vast and so diffuse that he rendered himself impotent as a writer. He had little sense of scholarly discipline, of the routine of note-taking and checking references. He could not therefore marshal his evidence and write with the confidence that he could easily supply chapter and verse.

Goulding Brown did not have this difficulty. He was meticulous about note-taking. He too read very widely, not only in history but also in theology (he had a fine collection of Newman first editions), classics, English literature and his two special interests: cricket and the antiquities of chess. He kept up his classical learning to the very end, setting himself lengthy portions of Greek verse to construe each Long Vacation. It helped to sharpen his mind, he told me. It would be quite wrong to suppose that his admiration for Gibbon and Maitland, and his choice of books for freshman to read, indicated an unwillingness to keep abreast with his subject. He read new books and special studies as they appeared – often, it must be said, with sadness at the manifest decline in the standards of English prose – and personally attended new courses of lectures on the subjects which he was teaching. He rarely missed a public lecture, and if obliged to do so, arranged for his wife to go in his stead so that she could take notes.

He knew what was being said, but was rarely convinced. Galbraith's studies on the compilation of the Domesday Book greatly fascinated him, and he brooded long over their significance. In the end, however, he withheld his complete approbation because he could not lightly abandon a position which had been defended by 'the genius of Maitland together with the pernicketiness of John Horace Round'. He read carefully and critically, frequently writing terse letters to eminent authors of the day to take them to task for infelicities of expression or to remind them of the insights exhibited by their more eminent forebears, and he would display their replies to his pupils. It grieved him not at all to be considered unfashionable.

Amongst his papers he left a series of jottings which he had compiled during his last years. He wrote thus on Max Beerhohm:

> Max was ... condemned for remaining a man of the 1890s, and for looking back nostalgically to the years before 1914. But I agree with him in taking no pleasure in the notion of the 'century of the common man'.

We also find this entry on T. S. Eliot:

> 'He was as careful of words as he was careful of everything else.' *Tablet*, Jan 9th, 1965, p.33. Was he? I find 'different than' in *The Sacred Wood* (p.122), and that in the second edition (1928). As a critic I find him wordy, pompous, empty. The *T.L.S.* (Jan. 7th, 1965, p.9) calls his criticism 'packed and graceful'. No, clumsy, rather. e.g. 'It (Matthew Arnold's writing) is still a bridge across the Channel, and it will always have been good sense.' As for his poetry, if I had been told that the author of *Prufrock* or *The Waste Land* was mad, I should not have doubted ... I feel a certain

sympathy with Eliot's view of Meredith. I decided long ago that he had no notion how to tell a story, and that his reputation for wisdom resulted from his saying very ordinary things in a complicated way. But I put forward this opinion with great submission, because I have against me A. W. Verral, whom I regard as the greatest literary critic writing in English since Coleridge.

Poles apart as they were in temperament and outlook, Welbourne and Goulding Brown had, nevertheless, certain significant points in common. They were both conscious of standing *contra mundum*. Goulding Brown, for instance, deplored the brashness and professionalism of much modern historical writing, especially since they were so often combined with carelessness in exposition. The trouble was that the young men took themselves too seriously. In his jottings he quotes Dr Johnson's famous words about the historian's moderate talents:

> Great talents are not requisite for an Historian; for in historical composition all the greatest powers of the human mind are quiescent. He has facts ready to his hand; so there is no exercise of invention. Imagination is not required in any high degree; only about as much as is used in the lower kinds of poetry. Some penetration, accuracy, and colouring will fit a man for the task, if he can give the application which is necessary.

Goulding Brown commented thus:

> Canon Charles Smyth once quoted this as a preface to a paper read to the C.U. Historical Society. It was received with derisive laughter. I could not join in that cachinnation. Surely there is only a shallow stream of thought in Macaulay, a little less shallow, perhaps, in G. M. Trevelyan, less shallow still in Gibbon. Maitland, indeed, is different; in him there is much real thought. Surely there is far less hard thinking in History than in physics, metaphysics, mathematics, or even in genuine (such as Housman's) textual criticism. What the historian does need is well stated by Walter Bagehot in his essay on Gibbon: 'Practical people have little idea of

the practical ability required to write a large book, and especially a large history.' Yes, certainly, practical ability, common sense, industry, far more than deep thought, are what is required.

I think that Welbourne would have agreed with much of this. In the letters which he wrote to me while I was out of Cambridge between 1954 and 1959, the contempt for modern attitudes to the study of history finds expression on almost every page. 'The high medievalists have made their subject into a mystery which will kill it', he wrote. He referred to many of his fellow-historians as 'technicians'; he was distrustful of the treatment of historiography (which he called 'the history of the history of the history of history') as a sort of science. We had gone blind to the real stuff of history, which he defined as 'who people were, not what people thought, but this is maybe because I can't think myself. I have been battling with the last four volumes of Toynbee, which I rashly accepted for review. It seems madness to me'. One should study philosophers only in order to see the extent to which intelligent people could be taken in. He wrote:

> I don't regard Bertram Russell as entirely right, but I remember my pleasure when I stumbled on his plain statement that he tested Hegel on the only field he himself then knew – mathematics – and found it nonsense, and found later a good deal more of it was nonsense ... yet it took in the world, as did Hitler also, and as do the Communists.

Professionalism led to a mystique, and mystique to romance. Too many historians, through lack of plain common sense and simple observation, missed the obvious and sold their own rationalisations as truth. Above all, they failed to look at the people who really mattered. B. L. Manning never fell into this error. He knew the people who mattered in Victorian England, and knew what mattered to them. 'The Victorian Liberal Party was religious not political', Welbourne once wrote to me, 'because only a few men get into a position in life where politics begin to apply. We must all believe even if we cheat ourselves by disbelieving.'

C. R. Fay was an historian whom Welbourne saluted. He had thought to study the rainfall figures during the years of the Chartist Movement and had been to Canada to see for himself the technique of prairie farming. He knew how the machines worked. All Welbourne's pupils were encouraged to study technology, a subject in which he himself was expert. I remember him talking over coffee for quite an hour on the history of hat making, following an idle inquiry about the headgear of the Mongols. This was real knowledge, and to find out the truth you might have to talk with a master-craftsman himself, which to Welbourne was sheer delight.

Welbourne admired 'a proper man' (his own chosen phrase) – a man like F. L. Allan, Headmaster of Wallasey Grammar School, who came up like himself from a humble background, who fished and walked and spoke his mind. He would laugh at Allan's story of the young German who went tramping with him over the Welsh hills and thought to walk the decrepit old man off his feet. After forty miles, mostly uphill, 'the deluded youth broke into tears'. There was no cant about Allan, 'none of the self-assertion or the ambition or the arrogance which a good many seem to need'. A man like this kept Welbourne's faith in human nature alive. He had little use for politicians, either of the Left ('a shabby lot of folk prancing in boots too big for them and frightened of their own success') or of the Right ('a set of businessmen disguised as gentlemen'). He much preferred rebels. In June 1956 he wrote to me:

> I shall go to Lincolnshire with a bag of books, and sit and pretend to read them, though I have read some, returning to my old love, Fenian history – the strange lie of England from 1848 onward that the Irish could be held in subjection, and the strange omission from history books of shall I say the Irish descent on Chester Castle

> under the leadership of a former American colonel – called off as the actual assault was – to seize the stock of arms, the Holywood packet, and then make a landing in Dublin where 6000 of the Irishmen in the garrison were sworn Fenians anyhow. I still believe that the attack would have succeeded, remembering Majuba and the like.

Being the man he was, he was bound 'to quarrel with almost every page' of Professor Brogan's *The English People*, which Dr Brittain, in a moment of inspiration, invited Welbourne to review for the *Cambridge Review* in November 1944. This I believe to be the only occasion when Welbourne allowed himself to write just as he talked, and it is therefore a document of peculiar interest.

> There's little omitted from this book but the People after whom it is named. Once a pale ghost of a Cockney appears, confounding a curate with a jest; he pops up again in another place because he has read G. B. Shaw. He must have learned his one word in some book. Here's an England where Chesterton is authority on the lack of English interest in equality, so well treasured by the Scots. Well, the last informed man from North of the Trent to whom I talked was looking forward to a return to worlds where Chesterton stayed with an O'Connor he called Brown. There Vice-Chancellors travelled by tram, and bought tickets from girls who addressed them as 'luv'. There schoolmasters are young girls, and not dominies in top hats.

He recalled an Oxford Professor who had exposed the futility of thinking of England as having something to do with Oxford Common Rooms and 'smart sherry parties near Sloane Square'. This man certainly 'knew a world where a half-heard remark about schools would bring the question: 'Eaton Mersey, or 'Eaton Moor?'

He then passed to the decline of militant and party songs:

Even General Booth couldn't make good use of the devil's songs of today. So we must wait until further revelations from the West, from the world which Puritan Fathers won for Bishop O'Leary to rule, send folk back to metrical psalms, to save the Bible under the aspidistra in every Council house from replacement by pictures of Stalin, or those photogravures of the last Italian Servant of the Servants of God which prove so completely that Calvinism ruined aesthetic taste.

There should be an honoured place in the world, and certainly at Cambridge, for a man who could think and talk like this. Yet Welbourne, even when he became Master of Emmanuel, could never come to terms with the Establishment. There was often a trace of bitterness in the occasional remarks which he would drop about his own past – something connected with a deep distrust of the London School of Economics and everything it stood for. He could give vent to harsh views of the world. In a letter of great length in which he inveighed against Oxford education and what he felt to be the scandalous inadequacy of *The Times* obituary on Lord Porter (Honorary Fellow of Emmanuel) – the two being connected in his mind – he commented as follows: 'The whole skill of the English has been in throwing to the wolves the other fellow so that the sledge could keep in front of the wolves, but I don't believe the present men are skilful enough to manage.'

Goulding Brown had, perhaps, more cause to feel some resentment against the academic world. A don to his fingertips, he never received official recognition. He saw his pupils go off to fellowships, headmasterships, lectureships and professional chairs, but little came his way by return. He applied for only two academic posts during his career; one was a Prize Fellowship at Trinity in 1906, when he was narrowly defeated by D. A. Winstanley, whose dissertation on 'Lord Chatham and the Whig Opposition' (subsequently published) was in the same field as his own. He then applied for a lectureship at Leeds, where he was defeated by G. M. Young. Thereafter Goulding Brown settled in Cambridge, lecturing during the First World War for the English Faculty on Donne, and subsequently becoming Seeley Librarian. He directed studies in History for Downing and Emmanuel: incomprehensibly, he was never offered a fellowship at either college. He was given rooms in Emmanuel, dining-rights and membership of the Parlour, but was denied the honour that would have meant so much.

It would have helped him if he had written and published; but Goulding Brown, purist as he was, was curiously diffident about his own prose style and looked upon the act of composition as a chore. His task was to read and to teach; to him, the most profitable and honourable activities. We may turn again to his jottings on Max Beerbohm:

> I am strongly for Max. He knew what he could do, and he did it. Dean Inge considered that it was 'really a good thing that a few able men should be content to be very leisurely'. Many of my favourites are people who wrote little – Sir Thomas Browne, Halifax ('the Trimmer'), Gray, W. Johnson Cory, Walter Raleigh, Max himself, A. E .Housman. Most people who write much, write too much.

Welbourne, like Goulding Brown, knew that writing was not his real medium. Short pieces – especially obituaries – he could do superbly. But with his teaching and his College duties as Senior Tutor and Master, he had little time for anything else. He once wrote to me:

> I ought to have written a book every two years, but I over-estimated the need for it to be a good book and watched poor books gaining other men reputations. I was as I know over-tired by my work, and as I know now, much more the worse for the 1914 war than I then knew.

So there is little by way of literary remains to pass to posterity, to stand as the memorial of these two great teachers. But then, as Maitland himself wrote of his mentor, Henry Sidgwick, in words which Goulding Brown would at once have recognised as the finest tribute ever paid by a grateful pupil to a revered master, ‘we need no memorial ... We cannot forget. Only in some way or another we could bear some poor testimony of our gratitude and our admiration, our reverence and our love.’

III

THE EMOTIVE NATURE OF VICTORIAN PROSE

This lecture was originally published in *Essays By Divers Hands,* Transactions of the Royal Society of Literature, New Series, Volume XLIV. I have made a few modifications to the original, especially the opening paragraph which recalled my debt to Bertram Goulding Brown in terms too reminiscent of my tribute to him in the preceding essay. I have also inserted a short passage which I decided to omit in the original lecture in order to keep within the prescribed time limit.

III

THE EMOTIVE NATURE OF VICTORIAN PROSE

The Don Carlos Memorial Lecture at the Royal Society of Literature, 10 October 1985

The most rigorous teacher to seize my youth as an undergraduate at Cambridge, reading for the History Tripos in the early 1950s, was a quaint and very elderly don, named Bertram Goulding Brown, the first twenty years of whose life had been spent in the reign of Queen Victoria. I think that his heart had ever remained in that age. As *laudator temporis acti* he was dogmatic and unashamed, and his admiration for the idols of his youth was exceeded only by his respectful contempt for the lack of sensitivity to language of those who came after them. It was his firm belief, for instance, that the finest literary critic writing in English since Coleridge was the classical scholar A. W. Verrall, an opinion which, I suspect, he advanced the more militantly after suffering from the ordeal of having F. R. Leavis as an undergraduate pupil. Gibbon once wrote of St Athanasius that 'the more he read, the less he comprehended'. With Goulding Brown it would be accurate to say that the more he read of modern authors, the less he could tolerate their brashness and slipshod style, and the more inhibited he himself became at putting pen to paper. So it was that a lifetime spent at Cambridge, reading and teaching for the History Tripos, left as its legacy of published work but two printed pages – an editorial supplied for a volume on the history of chess.

He taught me two things, however, for which I am eternally grateful. The first was a respect for the giants of historical writing – Gibbon, Macaulay, Freeman and above all, Maitland – on whose works his reading-lists tended to be based. Secondly, the essays that I tentatively produced for him week by week were subjected to the most meticulous and fastidious criticism of their style. Whether or not I proved an apt pupil of such teaching is neither here nor there; certainly I was maddeningly frustrated by his pedantry, which at times seemed almost insupportable. But the lesson was there to be learned, and it was a clear one. What you chose to say was assuredly no more important than how you chose to say it, and – in some ways – less so, because style is the man, and if you cannot express yourself lucidly and attractively, you betray discourtesy to your reader and exhibit the muddled nature of your mind.

As I grew to know him better in later years, when I returned to Cambridge as a don, Goulding Brown once vouchsafed to me the reflection that if he were advising a young student of history how to learn the art of writing, he would offer three particular passages of English prose to guide him. His first choice rather surprised me because it was not written by an historian, nor was the subject historical. It was the celebrated passage from Matthew Arnold's preface to the first series of *Essays in Criticism,* where he is writing, with tongue in cheek, yet with a tear in his eye, about his beloved Oxford: 'Beautiful city ... Adorable dreamer', closing with the words 'home of lost causes, and forsaken beliefs, and unpopular names, and impossible loyalties'. I need not quote this in full to an audience at the Royal Society of Literature, whose members must know it well. But his second choice may be less familiar, as it certainly was to me. I had expected Gibbon, or Macaulay or perhaps Maitland: but, no. He referred me to a passage from the first volume of James Anthony Froude's *History of England,* where the author describes, in terms which most modern historians would reject as sheer romanticism, the death of medievalism and the coming of modern times. As a piece of historical writing it is very dated, although not perhaps as dated as some moderns might maintain. It is well worth quoting in full:

> For, indeed, a change was coming upon the world, the meaning and direction of which even still is hidden from us, a change from era to

> era. The paths trodden by the footsteps of ages were broken up; old things were passing away, and the faith and the life of ten centuries were dissolving like a dream. Chivalry was dying; the abbey and the castle were soon together to crumble into ruins; and all the forms, desires, beliefs, convictions of the old world were passing away, never to return. A new continent had risen up beyond the western sea. The floor of heaven, inlaid with stars, had sunk back into an infinite abyss of immeasurable space; and the firm earth itself, unfixed from its foundations, was soon to be but a small atom in the awful vastness of the universe. In the fabric of habit which they had so laboriously built for themselves, mankind were to remain no longer. And now it is all gone – like an unsubstantial pageant faded; and between us and the old English there lies a gulf of mystery which the power of the historian will never adequately bridge. They cannot come to us, and our imagination can but feebly penetrate to them. Only among the aisles of the cathedrals, only as we gaze upon those silent figures sleeping on their tombs, some faint conceptions float before us of what these men were when they were alive; and perhaps in the sound of church bells, that peculiar creation of medieval age, which falls upon the ear like the echo of a vanished world.

All sorts of subtleties are contrived here in order to attain the rhetorical effect. The language of pathos is used to express the inherent pathos of a civilisation doomed to die; word inversion (one of the most effective tools of the rhetorician's craft) creates a hidden poetry in the prose, rendered the more effective by the allusion to *The Tempest* ('like an unsubstantial pageant faded'); in the interests of euphony, the conventional label 'the Middle Ages' becomes 'medieval age'; not 'the medieval age'. The cadence throughout is perfect, notably the soft rise and fall of the final sentence, descending – as all the best final sentences should – to a monosyllabic end: 'falls upon the ear like the echo of a vanished world'. There is not a trace of insincerity here. It is self-conscious 'over-writing', certainly, because the writer is deeply and genuinely moved by the idea of a dying civilisation, and he must make the heart of his reader respond.

Froude had fallen in love with an idea, and wrote emotively about it. In the next passage (Goulding Brown's third offering to his hypothetical student), the author has fallen in love with a scene. This is Ruskin, at the beginning of the second volume of *The Stones of Venice,* describing the approach to that city by gondola 'when first upon the traveller's sight opened...' a vista so breath-taking that his prose evokes all the intensity of poetry.

> Well might it seem that such a city had owed her existence rather to the rod of the enchanter, than the fear of the fugitive; that the waters which had encircled her had been chosen for the mirror of her state, rather than the shelter of her nakedness; and that all which in nature was wild or merciless – Time and Decay, as well as the waves and tempests – had been won to adorn her instead of to destroy, and might still spare, for ages to come, that beauty which seemed to have fixed for its throne the sand of the hour-glass as well as of the sea.

This is emotive writing, intended to enchant. It is, of course, a form of rhetoric. Nowadays we tend to use the word 'rhetoric' in a derogatory sense. We may dismiss a piece of writing as 'mere rhetoric' because we find it meretricious or insincere; the nakedness of the argument is so dressed up that it is given a weight that its content cannot properly warrant; the object is to flatter, to ingratiate or to cajole. In particular, we tend to apply the term to the histrionic and polemical exploitation of the spoken word, notably in political oratory (of which the late eighteenth century was perhaps the golden age) and in the seductive arts of the nineteenth-century preacher.

Both techniques translate readily from the platform or the pulpit into the prose of the period. The most obvious example of wild, indeed almost frenzied, rhetoric occurs in page after page of

Thomas Carlyle. Whether he is writing polemical articles or historical studies, Carlyle's prose is aggressively rhetorical in style, sometimes blatantly aping the language of the hustings, at others (and more frequently) lapsing into the phrases, tones and cadences of the pulpit orator, and most notably the Hell-fire preacher. John Holloway has made a study of Carlyle's rhetoric in his book *The Victorian Sage*, and one has to concede that some of the rhetorical devices employed are not without subtlety. He has a superb vocabulary, for instance for exhibiting the sham and the specious in the attitudes and stances that he dislikes, and the frequent recourse to Biblical language is often studied. Professor Teufelsdrockh in *Sartor Resartus* is wont to declare his views in a series of Biblical quotations; and the villainous – especially in Carlyle's historical works – evoke an extraordinary range of Gehenna-type imagery, which John Holloway describes as 'diabolisms'. Here, as an example, is a short passage from the chapter on the execution of Marie Antoinette taken from the most celebrated of Carlyle's histories:

> There are few Printed things one meets with, of such tragic, almost ghastly significance as those bald pages of the *Bulletin du Tribunal Revolutionnaire,* which bear title, *Trial of the Widow Capet*. Dim, dim, as if in disastrous eclipse; like the pale kingdoms of Dis! Plutonic Judges, Plutonic Tinville; encircled, nine times, with Styx and Lethe, with Fire-Phlegethon and Cocytus named of Lamentation! The very witnesses summoned are like Ghosts: exculpatory, inculpatory, they themselves are all hovering over death and doom ...

Now we may pass to a different type of rhetoric, but equally pulpit-inspired. The author is John Henry Newman, and the work is the *Essay on the Development of Christian Doctrine,* written at the moment of his decision to be received into the Roman Catholic Church and as his justification for doing so. I quote from the famous peroration at the conclusion of the whole piece; subtle, delicate and winning:

> And now, dear Reader, time is short, eternity is long. Put not from you what you have here found; regard it not as a mere matter of present controversy; set not out resolved to refute it, and looking about for the best way of doing so; seduce not yourself with the imagination that it comes of disappointment, or disgust, or restlessness, or wounded feeling, or undue sensibility, or other weakness. Wrap not yourself round in the association of years past; nor determine to be truth which you wish to be so, nor make an idol of cherished anticipations. Time is short, eternity is long.

This last passage is the very quintessence of rhetoric, because it is rhetorical both in what it says and how it says it. All Newman is actually stating at the end of the *Essay* is: 'Believe me, even if my conclusions are distasteful, because you will regret it in the long run if you don't'; only, of course, he expresses this with such charm that one wants to believe him, perhaps, in spite of oneself.

But rhetoric need not be quite as bald as this and yet still be rhetoric. Any writing which aims in its style at persuasiveness and values the art of verbal blandishment falls within the definition of the word. Furthermore, I believe this to be one of the highest qualities of Victorian prose. It is certainly of a piece with the period. 'Style is the man', we are told; but – more than that – style is the reflection of the age which produces the writer and conditions his audience to a particular type of approach. A cultivated, reasonably leisured, middle-class reading public, for whom the written word was the chief medium of communication (almost the only medium, apart from a weekly sermon at church), savoured a style which a later, more frenetic, age of wider literacy but less learning, would consider verbose. One might say that there was neither need nor expectation, among this class, of instant communication, with all the brashness and insensitivity to nuances of meaning that tend to go with it. The audience whom the Victorian prose-writer addressed expected their literature, even their journalism, to be expansive and challenging and asked not only to be intellectually stimulated but also to be emotionally moved.

Moreover, the prose style that we are considering belongs to an age that was far less specialist and technical in its language than the jargon of professional literature today. Much of the writing of the times in which we live veers between two rather unpleasing extremes. On the one hand, there is the highly technical specialist disquistion, concerned purely with factual content, without even the pretence of communicating to the non-specialist; on the other, there is the clipped and brash instant communication of modern journalism and much popular writing, which sacrifices both subtlety and charm to the demand for instant instruction or gratification.

Specialisation and the advance of technical knowledge have tended to render much of scientific, historical, critical, theological and philosophical writing today almost unreadable and unintelligible save to the few. It was not so in days past. The nineteenth century was perhaps the last age of what I can only describe as 'professional unprofessionalism', meaning by that an age when writers took themselves highly seriously in the profession of letters but refused to regard the intellectual areas that they presumed to write about as either beyond their competence to expound with lucidity or beyond the ability of cultured readers to understand. All branches of knowledge were inter-connected, each separate discipline ministering ultimately to the same fundamental truths. There were therefore no closed areas to an educated man, either for him to delve into or for him to assess critically from a standpoint of an intelligent and well-read observer of his times. The Bishop of Oxford (Samuel Wilberforce) undertook, for instance, the major review of Darwin's *Origin of Species* – not the best choice of reviewer, admittedly, as it turned out; a Newcastle banker (Thomas Hodgkin) chose in his leisure moments to write what became the classic – and monumental – history of the Barbarian invasions in the early Middle Ages; an Inspector of Schools (Matthew Arnold) felt no presumption in blithely publishing his own interpretations of biblical theology; and an eminent City man, again a banker (Walter Leaf), won universal acclaim for his edition of the *Iliad.* Here were cultivated, well-read men of letters, addressing themselves to an audience who, on the whole, shared a similar cultural background, compounded of Christian and classical literature, and whose ears were attuned to the leisurely and elegant style in which these books were written. Darwin's *Origin of Species* might have offended religious sensibilities, but its exposition accorded with the canons of lucidity and eloquence of the time. This is how that celebrated study concludes:

> It is interesting to contemplate an entangled bank, clothed with plants of many kinds, with birds singing on the bushes, with various insects flitting about, and with worms crawling through the damp earth, and to reflect that these elaborately constructed forms, so different from each other, and dependent on each other in so complex a manner, have all been produced by laws acting around us ... There is grandeur in this view of life, with its several powers, having been originally breathed by the Creator into a few forms or into one; and that, whilst this planet has gone cycling on according to the fixed law of gravity, from so simple a beginning endless forms most beautiful and most wonderful have been, and are being, evolved.

This is a beautiful piece of prose, emotionally stirring, and contains not a word that even an educated child could fail to understand.

I realise that I could be accused of being unrealistically nostalgic here. It is neither possible to put the clock back nor is it even remotely desirable. It is a truism that knowledge must advance, and inevitably that will lead to more and more specialisation. No one can doubt that civilisation has gained immeasurably. Nevertheless a careful study of the best of Victorian prose writers should exhibit three qualities in their work, which it is not impossible to emulate today. The first may not be a feature that immediately springs to mind, especially if one supposes, quite erroneously, that rhetoric is little more than a sort of cosmetic garnishing in order to make an argument seem more convincing. That quality is precision of language. In 1947, Miss Dorothy Sayers (surely one of the finer prose writers of the twentieth century) gave a lecture to a Vacation Course on Education at Oxford, choosing for her subject 'The Lost Tools of Learning', in which she argued forcefully for a return to the medieval pattern of education whereby students were first taught how to think and how to learn before their heads were stuffed full of factual information. She posed the following question:

> Is not the great defect of our education today ... that although we often succeed in teaching our pupils 'subjects' we fail lamentably ... in teaching them how to think? They learn everything except the art of learning. It is as though we had taught a child, mechanically and by rule of thumb, to play *The Harmonious Blacksmith* upon the piano, but had never taught him the scale or how to read music; so that, having memorised *The Harmonious Blacksmith,* he still had not the faintest notion how to proceed from that to tackle *The Last Rose of Summer.*

The medieval system of education – the Trivium and the Quadrivium – protected students from this kind of nonsense; because before a student could embark upon the learning of subjects (the Quadrivium), he had first to master the tools of learning, which were defined in the Trivium as Grammar, Dialectic and Rhetoric. Miss Sayers put it thus:

> First he [the pupil] learned a language; not just how to order a meal in a foreign language, but the structure of language, and hence of language itself – what it was, how it was put together and how it

> worked. Secondly, he learned how to use language: how to define his terms and make accurate statements; how to construct an argument and how to detect fallacies in argument [his own argument and other people's]. Dialectic, that is to say, embraced Logic and Disputation. Thirdly, he learned to express himself in language [Rhetoric]; how to say what he had to say elegantly and persuasively.

The nineteenth century was nearer to the Middle Ages than we are, in more senses than the purely chronological. For reasons far too complex to explore here, it was nearer in its temper of mind, its priorities, its *Zeitgeist*, and its appreciation of the superiority of wisdom to knowledge than was the early eighteenth century, the so-called 'Age of Reason'. In general terms, its educational philosophy of 'Godliness and Good Learning' was, I believe, a sounder base for understanding one's world, and particularly for understanding one's world in the context of eternity, than anything that immediately preceded it and, I fear, than anything that came after it; and in the discipline of study at the universities, some of the best features of the old Trivium and Quadrivium had been preserved. The dominance of the Mathematical and Classical Triposes at Cambridge, and the Honour School of *Literæ Humaniores* ('Greats') at Oxford may have threatened to bind the clerisy of this country to an anachronism, but ensured – in compensation – a sound training in the tools of learning. Above all, they encouraged an appreciation of precision in both language and argument, most notably in those nurtured on Oxford Greats. The supreme example, to my mind, is John Henry Newman: *anima naturaliter Christiana,* child of Romanticism and Prize Fellow of that Oxford College that allegedly 'stank of logic' (Oriel), so that the combination of the deep spirituality, emotional power and precision in the art of disputation made of him perhaps the most devastating, and the most subtle, of all nineteenth-century polemicists. We may take this passage from his essay on the Tamworth Reading Room in

Discussions and Arguments to see all these elements in play together:

> Science gives us the grounds or premises from which religious truths are to be inferred; but it does not set about inferring them, much less does it reach the inference; that is not its province. It brings before us phenomena, and it leaves us, if we will, to call them works of design, wisdom, or benevolence; and further still, if we will, to proceed to confess an Intelligent Creator. We have to take its facts, and to give them a meaning, and to draw our own conclusions from them. First comes knowledge, then a view, then reasoning, then belief. This is why Science has so little of a religious tendency; deductions have no power of persuasion. The heart is commonly reached, not through the reason, but through the imagination, by means of direct impressions, by the testimony of facts and events, by history, by description. Persons influence us, voices melt us, looks subdue us, deeds inflame us. Many a man will live and die upon a dogma; no man will be a martyr for a conclusion.

And one further example: the most moving paragraph in the whole of the *Apologia,* structurally perfect, with the most sensitive use of contrasting sentence length, falling at its conclusion to a simple sentence of four monosyllables. The sentiment is characteristic too, for Newman is explaining the subordinate position of logic in the most important decisions that a man may have to take.

> I had a great dislike of paper logic. For myself, it was not logic that carried me on; as well might you say that the quicksilver in the barometer changes the weather. It is the concrete being that reasons; pass a number of years, and I find my mind in a new place: how? The whole man moves; paper logic is but the record of it. All the logic in the world would not have made me move faster towards Rome than I did; as well might you say that I have arrived at the end of my journey, because I see the village church before me, as venture to assert that the miles, over which my soul had to pass

> before it got to Rome, could be annihilated, even though I had been in possession of some far clearer view than I then had, that Rome was my ultimate destination. Great acts take time.

This passage repays reading over and over again to savour the perfection of the cadence. And cadence is the second quality of nineteenth-century emotive prose that I would strongly commend. Newman actually tells us where he learned the art. At the age of seventeen he was introduced to the writings of Gibbon: 'I fell in love with the twelfth volume of Gibbon, and my ears rang with the cadence of his sentences, and I dreamed of it for a night or two. Then I began to write an analysis of Thucydides in Gibbon's style.'

This is worth taking a little further. Matthew Arnold once observed that a perfect sentence is one that passes the test of 'inevitability'; that is to say the choice of words and their sequence are so patently right that, were one to change a single syllable, the magic would be lost. Gibbon passes this test time and time again. G. M. Young, in his short biography of Gibbon, supplies a good example in the following passage from that writer's acknowledged masterpiece:

> The slave of Imperial despotism, whether he was condemned to drag his gilded chains in Rome and the senate, or to wear out a life of exile on the barren rock of Seriphus or the frozen banks of the Danube, expected his fate in silent despair. To resist was fatal; and it was impossible to fly.

'This is spoken prose', Young writes. 'It needs to be read aloud ... and if anyone will make the experiment of substituting "To resist was fatal: to fly was impossible", he will understand something of what oratory was on a night when Burke was speaking and Gibbon was listening.'

So the nineteenth-century writers had models to emulate in Burke and Gibbon. G. M. Young is surely right, too, in recommending the exercise of testing cadence by reading aloud. I recall a conversation I had some years ago with Rachel Trickett, Principal of St Hugh's, when we were jointly examining a DPhil thesis at Oxford. She admitted to having a highly sensitive ear to the rhythm and rise and fall of sentences in her own reading and writing, and explained how this had come about. Her father had been a Nonconformist minister, and as a child she had been taken regularly to hear him preach on Sundays. She remembered nothing of the content of the sermons, but the sound of the voice remained – the musical quality of his diction and his delicate turn of phrase. She recalled that on Sunday evenings, she and the other children in the family were allowed to remain in the drawing-room until quite late, the only rule imposed upon them being the stipulation that they must sit quietly by the fire, reading if they wished or drawing; and while the children were thus occupied, their father would read aloud from some great classic of literature. Macaulay was his favourite choice. After a while, the children would sleepily push aside their books and listen to their father's melodious voice, not understanding much of the adult language, but yielding nonetheless to the seductive sonorousness of the perfectly moulded sentences, beautifully read. So were their ears trained, painlessly and almost unconsciously, to sensitivity to cadence in writing.

I suspect that this was a common Victorian experience. Reading aloud was a frequent evening diversion in middle-class families; and the obligation of listening to weekly sermons, often enough losing the drift but still responding to the carefully studied diction, was almost universal. There is no doubt, for instance, that Matthew Arnold acquired his own mastery of rhetorical techniques from listening, at a very receptive stage of his life, to two very different but equally consummate preachers – his own father in Rugby Chapel and John Henry Newman from the pulpit of St Mary's.

That this attention to cadence by practitioners of the art themselves was a conscious element in their technique has at least one other childhood memory to stand as evidence. I remember hearing a talk on the radio several years ago by the daughter of F. W. Maitland. She looked back on the last days of Maitland's life, when he had to retire to the Channel Islands for the sake of his health. He wrote prolifically during these years, chiefly his articles on the highly technical subject of the history and origins of Trusts and Corporations. His daughter's memory of her father, whose study was directly above the room she occupied, was a most vivid recollection of hearing him write. She could hear him speaking out aloud each sentence as he shaped it, pacing the room; then, when satisfied, he would walk briskly to the writing-table, and his daughter would hear the chair being drawn back, followed by the 'scritch-scritch-scritch' of pen on paper. The pacing would then resume.

The mention of Maitland brings me to my third and final quality; and it is courtesy. Very early in my own writing career, while working on my first book, I was given by Sir Harold Nicholson what I believe to be not only good advice in itself but a precept which lies at the root of successful rhetoric as it was understood by the finest writers of the nineteenth century. 'Remember', he said, 'that your first problem is to determine the nature of the audience you are addressing. Thereafter you must be consistent in your mode of communicating with them.' The best rhetoric is not wordy self-indulgence or florid ornamentation; it is honouring your obligation to your reading public of being intelligible, and – as far as possible – attractively so. Lytton Strachey once observed that the significance of Wordsworth's preface to *Lyrical Ballads* was that he taught his generation 'the innate aesthetic value possessed by extreme simplicity'. I believe this to have been the particular genius of Maitland as a writer and as an historian too. He was a deeply courteous man. He would never presume, for instance, to savage another scholar with whose views he found himself in disagreement. ‘An erring colleague’, he once wrote, ‘is not an Amalakite to be smitten hip and thigh’. More than that, he aimed always to explain the exceedingly complex subjects on which he chose to write, chiefly – as is well known – studies within the history of English medieval law. Indeed, the more technical and arid his subject, the lighter and simpler would be his prose. A fine example of his style comes at the conclusion of the first chapter of *Domesday Book and Beyond,* where he describes his quest for simplicity as part of the historical process:

> Unless we have mistaken the general drift of legal history, the law implied in *Domesday Book* ought to be for us a very difficult law, far more difficult than the law of the thirteenth century, for the thirteenth century is nearer to us than the eleventh. The grown man will find it easier to think the thoughts of the school-boy than to think the thoughts of a baby. And yet the doctrine that our remote forefathers being simple folk had simple law dies hard. Too often we allow ourselves to suppose that, could we but get back to the beginning, we should find that all was intelligible, and then should be able to watch the process whereby simple ideas were smothered under subtleties and technicalities. But it is not so. Simplicity is the outcome of technical subtlety; it is the goal, not the starting-point. As we go backwards, the familiar outlines become blurred; the ideas become fluid; and instead of the simple we find the indefinite. But difficult though our task may be, we must turn to it.

Throughout this paper I have spoken of rhetoric as practically synonymous with style; or, at least, with an emotive style which self-consciously seeks to please and captivate the reader. Perhaps in drawing the occasional comparison with the modern age I have been guilty of making my contrasts too stark. There is, for instance, a whole genre of twentieth-century writing, especially in the field of *belles-lettres,* where the exercise of weaving spells of verbal blandishment produced prose writers of the very highest distinction and sensitivity – a *petit-maître* like

Max Beerbohm, a controversialist like Lytton Strachey, a languorous master of technique like Percy Lubbock. But the rise and fall of the art of *belles-lettres* is a subject in itself. One particular irony strikes me, however, when I compare the present with the nineteenth-century past, and it is this: how odd it is that an age which has become so conscious of the need to communicate at all levels should have become so artless in the means by which it strives so to do. It has a lot to do with democracy, of course; with the coming of almost universal literacy; with the acceleration of the whole pace of life; and with the predominance of the aural and visual media. But it is no bad thing occasionally to ponder a little on the price which we have had to pay in the process, and to lament what we have lost.

Society changes, and art is the expression of that change. Contemporary art forms are, and have been now for several decades, severely intellectual, making no concession to viewer or auditor or reader. It is as if the *Zeitgeist* of the late twentieth century commanded that all serious art should be deeply introspective; and that any attempt to enthral must seem to belittle the profundity of its message or to diminish the sincerity of its tone. The Victorians would not, I think, have understood this. Even the deadly serious writer, with a challenging social message, strove to appeal to the heart as well as the head. If a group of intelligent six-formers today were asked to supply the names of the five serious and widely-read contemporary authors whom they would select at the top of their reading-list, I wonder how their answers would compare with the choice of their equivalents 130 or so years ago, had the same question been put to them. Fortunately we have historical evidence to help us here. A Royal Commission in 1860 put this very question to an undergraduate: what did he read at school? The answer was as follows: 'Scott, Dickens, Macaulay, Tennyson; Kingsley, of course.'

'Kingsley, of course': what a curious choice, we might say. But, no; Kingsley was the stirrer of youthful conscience, and it was as necessary to read him then as it is for an intelligent boy to read – well, whom? – today. Golding, perhaps; Camus, maybe?

When Kingsley himself was asked to explain his vogue among the young and the clerisy of the future (the questioner had *Hypatia* particularly in mind), he gave an answer which perhaps sums up the whole argument of my piece. He did not say, 'I have a message', or 'I agonise, therefore I must be taken seriously.' He pointed at once to the rhetorical technique, something with which he had been born. To use his own words: 'I have a certain knack of utterance', he said, and added, 'nothing but a knack.'

IV

THOMAS ARNOLD: A BICENTENARY APPRAISAL

The Thomas Arnold Memorial Lecture to mark the bicentenary of his birth was given in the Examination Schools at Oxford on 7 November 1995, at the invitation of the Provost and Fellows of Oriel College. [This lecture was published in 2005 by the Catholic Record Society in *Victorian Churches and Churchmen: Essays presented to Vincent Alan McClelland*, edited by Sheridan Gilley. We are grateful for permission to reproduce it here.]

IV

THOMAS ARNOLD: A BICENTENARY APPRAISAL

The Oriel College Thomas Arnold Memorial Lecture, 7 November 1995, in the Examination Schools, Oxford

The final entry in Thomas Arnold's diary, dated 11 June 1842, two days before his 47th birthday, contains the following reflection: 'How large a portion of my life on earth is already passed ... Still there are works which, with God's permission, I could do before the night cometh.'[1] Twelve hours later he was dead. Like his father before him – a Customs Officer on the Isle of Wight – who died when Thomas was only six; like, too, both his brothers who died before middle age, his life was cut short in its prime. This is worthy of record because we are apt to look upon Arnold as one of the most eminent of 'Eminent Victorians' (notoriously designated as such, indeed, for the purpose of calculated ridicule by Lytton Strachey), when actually barely five years of his life were passed during Victoria's reign. There are, however, good grounds for allowing the label to stand; not only because so many of the attitudes and tensions which we tend to regard as quintessentially 'Victorian' long antedated the accession of the Queen in 1837, and were abundantly evident in the person of Arnold himself, but also because Arnold's influence was arguably greater after his death than before it. As A. O. J. Cockshut has put it: 'He was not a Victorian, but he trained Victorians ... in an odd way he seems more typical of the decade that followed his death than of any period in his own lifetime.'[2]

Many reasons can be advanced to explain the emergence and expanding influence of the moral idealism which lay at the root of what came to be known as 'Arnoldianism'. Echoes of their Master's voice could be plainly heard from the lips of 'the Doctor's Disciples' – those who had sat at Arnold's feet in his highly-privileged Sixth Form and had acted as his Præposters;

more so at Oxford than at Cambridge, because the more ancient University had always been Arnold's preferred destination for his most favoured pupils. Their veneration for their old Headmaster and the self-conscious high moral stance they adopted was certainly noticed and commented upon, if not always commended: there being uneasy suspicions of moral priggishness. Rather more significant, however, was the studied application of Arnoldian methods followed by former members of his staff, like George Cotton at Marlborough and James Prince Lee at King Edward's Birmingham, or by an ex-pupil like C. J. Vaughan at Harrow, all of whom served to pass on the Arnoldian legacy to those who were to become the headmasters of the many new public-school foundations of the 1850s and 1860s.

Only two years after Arnold's death, George Moberly, Headmaster of Winchester, acknowledged the nature of this legacy in the following words:

> A most singular and striking change has come upon our public schools – a change too great for any person to appreciate adequately, who has not known them in both these times ... I am sure that to Dr Arnold's personal earnest simplicity of purpose, strength of character, power of influence and piety, which none who ever came near him could mistake or question, the carrying of this improvement into our schools is mainly attributable. He was the first.[3]

It is no unusual phenomenon that a man has to wait until his death before he gains popular acclaim. During his Rugby years Arnold was known – and often attacked – as an outspoken polemicist; and there was a period in the mid-1830s when the decline of numbers in the school reflected public concern over both his religious views and his handling of certain disciplinary issues. Unexpected public recognition came in 1841 when Lord Melbourne, in a rare moment of inspiration, offered Arnold the Regius Professorship of Modern History at Oxford. At the same time, his published sermons were beginning to make a deep impression upon the reading public, whose appetite for such fare – in contrast to our own day – might almost be described as voracious. The Queen read them with approval, we are told.[4] Gladstone, rather surprisingly – in view of his admiration for Newman's Anglican sermons[5] – declared that Arnold's were his special favourite.[6]

As is well known, however, two books, published in 1844 and 1857 respectively, ensured that Arnold's name would become a household word. Arthur Stanley, later Dean of Westminster and Arnold's most devoted disciple, received the commission to write the official 'Memoir'. When he saw the papers that had been made available to him, he wrote in his journal: 'If I am not able to make out of them one of the most remarkable biographies that has appeared for a long time, it will be my fault, not theirs.'[7] He need not have worried. By Christmas 1844, the book had gone through four editions in almost as many months. The hero-worship was barely disguised, but that seemed hardly to matter to the many who found the celebrated account of Arnold's work and ideals at Rugby – in the long third chapter – totally absorbing by its revelation of the trials and challenges of one man's mission to create a Christian community out of such unpromising material as a potentially wayward and indifferent society of boys. But there was more to Arnold than this. When Charles Dickens was sent extracts from Arnold's letters, deploring the cruelty of the new Poor Law, he became a convert on the instant. 'I must have that book', he wrote. 'Every sentence that you quote from it is the text-book of my faith.'[8] (One wonders if he noticed another letter of Arnold's, in which he blamed the influence of books 'like Pickwick, Nickleby, Bentley's magazine, &c &c' for encouraging 'childishness' in boys).[9]

Thirteen years after Stanley's *Life*, Thomas Hughes published his *Tom Brown's Schooldays*, scoring even greater success than Stanley, for this was a book which sold in its thousands both in England and in America. The hero of the story is a boy just like Hughes himself (or as Hughes recalled of himself at Rugby) – an ordinary, decent, not particularly clever, quite unpriggish, outdoor sort of boy. But Arnold is a hero, too, seen from the more distant vantage point of a boy who was never – unlike Stanley – one of the Doctor's elite, and therefore what he absorbed from Arnold's teaching and his Sunday sermons on moral courage and Christian virtues, was a simplified (and – in Stanley's opinion – distorted) distillation of Arnold's ideals. It is easy to see how exhortations to Christian manliness, which to Arnold and Stanley were understood in a Pauline sense, could be translated into something that spoke directly to a boy's admiration for the robust and the physical; in a phrase – 'Muscular Christianity'. E. C. Mack puts it thus:

> Hughes's Arnold has neither the fanatic idealism, the other-worldliness, nor the over-developed sense of sin that the real Arnold possessed. He has become a glorified boy scoutmaster whose strenuous spirituality has been made palatable to Englishmen by presenting it under the guise of the honest manliness of a Kingsley hero.[10]

So – less then twenty years after his death – it was becoming increasingly difficult to disentangle the Arnold of history from the legendary figure that his greatest admirers were tending to make of him.

Nevertheless this is what we must now attempt to do. What was he actually like? Of his absolute integrity, no one can seriously doubt. As a young fellow of Oriel (he was elected at the age of 20), he went through a period of agonising doubts over proceeding to Orders because he felt that he could not subscribe wholeheartedly to certain of the Articles of Religion (especially on the nature of the Trinity). It is probably true to say that in the end he stifled these doubts rather than resolved them; but at least he displayed his honesty by careful avoidance of dogmatic preaching thereafter. One early critic (in 1827, when Arnold was still engaged in private tutoring at Laleham) said of him that he suffered from the 'fault of an unsubmissive understanding'.[11] To the accusation of arrogance, levelled at him in 1829, when he had been defending Catholic Emancipation on historical grounds, he gave a lofty reply which hardly exonerates him of the charge: 'I do not consider it to be arrogant', he wrote, 'to assume that I know more of a particular subject, which I have studied eagerly from a child, than those do who notoriously do not study it at all.'[12] He frankly admitted to being ambitious. 'I believe that, naturally, I am one of the most ambitious men alive', he confessed to a Rugby pupil who was seeking advice on a profession, while adding that only ambitions worthy of the name were to become prime minister, or a governor of a great empire, 'or the writer of works which should live in every age and every country'.[13] A letter of July 1836 to his friend Sir John Franklin, recently appointed Governor of Van Diemen's Land, is altogether more revealing, however. He would be strongly tempted to accompany him to that unhappy convict settlement – as the bishop, perhaps, or the principal of a college – because in such a capacity he could assist 'in forming the moral and intellectual character of a new society'.[14] Although the letter continues with sentiments that reveal a painful lack of sympathy for the convict population, at least Arnold had accurately stated what his true aspirations were. If the day came that his work at Rugby had been accomplished, he would seek other realms to conquer, not for the glory of high rank but for the satisfaction of doing a good and lasting Christian work; to repeat the Rugby experiment elsewhere, in fact.

There was one quality above all that enabled him to exercise such an influence over others: earnestness. It was Bonamy Price, commenting on Arnold's relationship with his little coterie of pupils at Laleham, who first discerned it.

> Dr Arnold's great power as a private tutor resided in this, that he gave such an intense earnestness to life. Every pupil was made to

feel that there was a work for him to do – that his happiness as well as his duty lay in doing that work well.[15]

And there, in those two sentences, we have it all. The three words – earnestness, work, duty. They are the words that come, perhaps, first to our minds when we try to describe the dominant ethic of the mid-Victorian period, the prosperous noontide of nineteenth-century England, which Arnold never lived to see. Longfellow, in his 'Psalm of Life', translated Arnoldianism into verse:

Life is real! Life is earnest!
And the grave is not its goal:
Dust thou art, to dust returnest,
Was not spoken of the soul.[16]

Life was certainly for action. Arnold wanted his pupils to be 'up and doing'. But again we return to the ambiguity of interpretation. As Norman Vance points out, Arnold's ideal was really 'a self-reliant moral maturity which recalls the Coleridgean ideal of self-superintendant virtue'.[17] We may doubt that Thomas Hughes the Rugbeian would have understood language like this. To him, and probably many like him, Arnold's message suggested something more actively heroic – a call to the standard under which 'Christian soldiers' would be called to serve 'for the benefit of the whole nation'.[18]

We are back in the world of Tom Brown again. When Fitzjames Stephen reviewed the book, he made the shrewd observation that what Arnold 'and his admirers' had achieved was 'the substitution of the word "earnest" for its predecessor "serious"'.[19] 'Seriousness' was one of the key words of nineteenth-century Evangelicalism, and to them it bore a technical meaning. The possession of the quality of 'seriousness' meant that you were a 'real' Christian as opposed to a 'nominal' Christian; and one of the hallmarks of a 'serious' Christian was that you exhibited a sort of joyousness in the Lord on every possible occasion, thereby proclaiming your favoured status to the world at large. Arnold was not an Evangelical and would not have used this language. But he was not by nature a solemn man. Bonamy Price has supplied the following slightly improbable picture of him, relaxing with his pupils at Laleham:

> Who that ever had the happiness of being at Laleham, does not remember the lightness and joyousness of heart, with which he would romp and play in the garden, or plunge with a boy's delight into the Thames: or the merry fun with which he would battle with spears with his pupils.[20]

This is one of those vignettes which remind us from time to time that the distance between our own day and the nineteenth century seems measured in light years. I would suggest that another instance occurred earlier. I cannot conceive any headmaster of the present day doing other than rejoice at the prospect of boys reading Dickens for pleasure. Similarly the image of adults 'romping' or 'frolicking' in the way that Bonamy Price describes seems to us more than faintly risible; or if not that, then perhaps 'childish'. One has to remember, however, that of the outdoor games Victorian (and pre-Victorian) adults were wont to play in their lighter moments, a favourite appears to have been leap-frog! After all, Mr Pickwick was tempted to discard his greatcoat on one sunny afternoon and to persuade Mr Tupman to show his back for just such a game.[21] Thomas Hughes and J. M. Ludlow occasionally invited students of the London Working Men's College to join them for Sunday lunch at their house in Wimbledon, concluding with games of leap-frog in the garden.[22] Two future Archbishops of Canterbury – E. W. Benson, then Master of Wellington, and Frederick Temple, Headmaster of Rugby – together with Charles Kingsley tried collectively to raise the spirits of the first group of Foundationers at Wellington in 1859 by setting an example of sportive play. Temple punted a football about 'wildly', we are told; and Kingsley – quite in character – set in motion a game of leap-frog.[23] One suspects that when everybody else had tired, Kingsley was still leaping higher and more vigorously then the rest. Of all the pictures of Victorian worthies relaxing out-of-doors, however, my favourite is Arthur Benson's description of the solemn Bishop of Durham, Brooke Foss Westcott, on holiday with the Bensons at the seaside. 'On a hot summer afternoon we sat by the sea, and a cock-shy was set up. Westcott threw stones at it, with a deadly intentness, far harder and quicker than anyone else.'[24] This was near the nineteenth century's end; but it is a faithful picture of earnestness in play.

All this, however, is to digress. A man of passionate beliefs, whose conception of his appointment to the headmastership of Rugby in December 1827 was that of a personal mission to turn a potential nursery of vice into a model of a Christian community, was not likely to brook any opposition. He was determined to fulfil what Edward Hawkins predicted of him in his testimonial to the Trustees – 'to change the face of education all through the public schools of England'.[25] As Michael McCrum has pointed out, this was a pretty meaningless phrase at the time. There were only seven such schools in 1827 and most of these studiously avoided deference to Arnold's work, Eton more so than any other.[26] In the long run, however – while admitting to an element of hyperbole – his prediction was not that far off the mark. It will seem strange to us that the Trustees appointed Arnold as Dr Wooll's successor without even an interview; strange too – although it was to have great significance in elevating the status of headmasters generally – that the Trustees acceded to Arnold's condition that he be given an entirely free hand, without any interference. They might dismiss him, if dissatisfied; otherwise they were to hold their peace. When the Earl Howe presumed, as an individual Trustee, to demand an open admission from the Headmaster that he was the author of his notorious unsigned denunciation of the Tractarians in the

Edinburgh Review, Arnold's response was one of the frostiest rebuffs ever penned.[27]

Indeed, Arnold could display an element of ruthlessness at times. His educational principles were, on the whole, admirable. Anyone who has had experience of schools will testify to the corrupting influence of a single vicious boy. Arnold's answer was to root out all such threats by expulsion. To encourage co-operation from his staff, which he did by regular three-weekly meetings with them and by confirming his respect for them by substantially improving the salary scale, was surely right. One of his major changes for the better was the abolition of 'dames'' houses and the appointment of housemasters to exercise direct pastoral supervision of their boys. Underlying all his policy at Rugby was his firm conviction that a Christian school should operate on the principle of mutual trust, and this he sought to achieve through his relations with his Sixth Form who were to be his exemplars in setting the whole moral tone of the school. On the whole that trust was repaid, although doubtless Arnold would have bridled at the cynicism implicit in the well-known maxim that if you fail to trust boys they will do you down, and if you trust them they will – being only boys – sometimes let you down. One particular responsibility, however, he safeguarded in his own person. From 1831 he took over the chaplaincy of the school, so that only his voice should be heard from the pulpit each Sunday. This was to be his most cherished vehicle for the transmission of his ideal of moral purification, and we know from the testimony of his youthful auditors over the years that these twenty-minute addresses – never longer – made a deep and enduring impression.

I think that it would be generally conceded that reliance upon Press reports for an accurate picture of the occasional dramas that spice the life of a public school would constitute a somewhat rash declaration of faith. This, nevertheless, has been the misguided temptation of certain historians, and most notably Professor T. W. Bamford, in efforts to confirm a suspicion that A.

P. Stanley's idol must have had feet of clay.[28] Even more misguided, however, has been the failure to realize that Arnold, because of his outspoken political writings, had made an inveterate enemy of the Tory Press, who seized eagerly upon every opportunity to vilify his reputation. This is the conclusion of a recent PhD thesis for the University of Hull by Dr Anthony Reeve who has conducted an exhaustive search for unpublished Arnold letters and papers, and has succeeded in making the most significant contribution to studies of Arnold as an educationalist since Stanley's *magnum opus*.

Dr Reeve does not maintain that Arnold never made a mistake. It was unfortunate that he flogged a boy called Marsh for lying when in fact he had been telling the truth, but he had no reason to suppose that the master who had reported the boy had himself made a mistake, a fact that did not come to light until 48 hours later. Arnold responded in the only honourable way; he made a public apology, wrote to the parents and received in return an expression of entire confidence in his conduct as headmaster, so that there was no question of their son being withdrawn. The Tory Press pounced upon another instance of alleged injustice – the expulsion of Nicholas Marshall, claiming, on the unsupported evidence of the aggrieved father, that the boy had been denied any opportunity to state his own case over an incident which could be represented as a gross abuse of power by the Præposters.[29] Correspondence which Dr Reeve has unearthed reveals that this was simply untrue. Marshall was certainly seen by Arnold after the offence had been reported to him. The boy, furthermore, admitted to taunting the Præposters, who had intervened to quell a disturbance in which he had been a central figure, and – instead of exercising his right to appeal – he had refused to accept punishment and had come to blows with three of the Præposters. It is difficult to see what else Arnold could have done other than remove him from the school.

The Wratislaw case of 1839 (so named after the local solicitor who initiated proceedings against the school) has also been re-examined by Dr Reeve in the light of new evidence. This at the time received wide publicity injurious to Arnold's reputation, when the Trustees were taken to court for alleged breach of the original charitable foundation of Lawrence Sheriff, intended to supply local boys with free education, it being further maintained that Arnold had deliberately put every possible obstacle in the way of these Foundationers proceeding from the Lower to the Upper School. Although the Trustees were exonerated on two counts, this last charge went undefended and judgment was found against them. It is now clear, however, that the Counsel for the Trustees, either through dilatoriness or through lack of awareness of the seriousness of the issue, failed to send Arnold the relevant affidavits, so that he was given no opportunity to state his own case, which he was confident would have adequately answered all the allegations against him.[30]

What was the long-term influence of Arnold's work at Rugby? In the first place he took what at the time were considered to be radical steps in the reform of the Rugby curriculum. These were not, however, in the direction of introducing a serious study of the sciences, for which neglect Corelli Barnett has – not entirely fairly – blamed him and the short-sightedness on the part of the headmasters who slavishly followed his methods for the lamentable failure to perceive the country's needs for scientific and technical education, thereby contributing to the loss of England's industrial supremacy in the later decades of the century. Arnold's reforms were within the traditional field of the study of the Classics, which had hitherto been largely Latin-based, involving the sentencing of generations of boys to the stultifying exercise of composing Latin verse.

Arnold's aim as a teacher was to imbue his pupils with his own passion for the historians and philosophers of Ancient Greece, notably Thucydides, Plato and Aristotle. 'The results of the reorientation, which was so clearly in keeping with the tendencies of the age', Robert Ogilvie has written, 'were to prove of incalculable benefit ... To Arnold is due much of the credit for originating the change.'[31] This aspect of Arnoldianism, rightly so described because what Arnold began at Rugby was followed by almost all his disciples in other schools, had its effect in the shaping of the *Literæ Humaniores* School at Oxford. 'By 1866', Ogilvie continues, 'every Oxford Greats man would be reading Plato and Thucydides, and nearly everyone at Oxford was reading Greats'.[32] This may not seem, especially to non-classicists, to be of earth-shattering importance, one must admit. What Ogilvie would seem to be claiming, however, is that Oxford at least was not unmoved by the change of direction in classical studies at school level, inaugurated by Arnold – a rare instance, perhaps, of the tail wagging the dog. And the text of Thucydides that was studied was Arnold's own scholarly edition. In his preface to the third edition of that work, he concluded with a passage that succinctly summed up his whole approach to the study of history, of which we must say more later. The work on which he had been engaged, he said, was not 'an idle enquiry about remote ages and forgotten institutions, but a living picture of things present, fitted not so much for the curiosity of the scholar as for the instruction of the statesman and the citizen'.[33]

G. M. Young has claimed that 'Arnold reconciled the serious classes to the public schools'.[34] What this really means is that it was Arnold's good fortune to articulate – whether consciously or not – a corpus of ideals and an ethical code which precisely matched what so many of his contemporaries believed were the particular needs of their times. Harold Perkin, for instance, has suggested that this was essentially an appeal to the changing society of the early nineteenth century and especially to what he describes as the 'entrepreneurial' classes, who liked what they saw, or what they read about, of Arnold's work at Rugby, not least the encouragement of the competitive spirit. To express it thus, I feel, is somewhat misleading. Arnold rejoiced in the successes of his pupils, but consistently placed the formation of character above the goal of academic success. He would never have approved of 'league tables' of schools. Perkin does, however, concede that Arnold's moral teaching and his ideal of gentlemanly conduct lay at the root of his appeal to this same class. 'His concept of the Christian gentleman was not that of the old chevalier, jealous of his paramilitary honour, but otherwise indifferent to morality', he writes, 'but that of the new "gentle" gentleman, competing not in duels but in consideration for others.'[35]

What we are seeing is the gradual coming-into-being of a common ethic, as the different classes of society come more and more to speak as one. This is a process that antedates Arnold's work at Rugby and probably owes more to the Evangelical Revival than to any other cause. It is interesting, for instance, to note Alexis de Tocqueville's account of a conversation with Edward Bulwer (the future Lord Lytton) in 1833 – too early a date for Arnold's influence to have been felt. Bulwer observes that 'there has been an immense revolution in the minds of Englishmen during the last half-century'. He predicts the decline of the aristocracy, noting that common dangers are bringing classes together to seek a common solution.[36] Gertrude Himmelfarb, writing in our own times, comments on the same phenomenon as follows: 'For the first time, a substantial part of the aristocracy and of the working-classes (and in each case the most influential part) shared the ideals and values of the middle classes.'[37] Some thirty-five years ago, when I first ventured into print on the subject of Arnoldianism, I described these ideals in the time-honoured phrase of John Colet: 'Godliness and Good Learning'. I am happy to let that stand.

By no means were all Arnold's public utterances received at the time with acclaim.[38] He was a compulsive writer. 'I must write or die', he used frequently to say. Furthermore, he was a man of restless energy, living – it seems – under a 'permanent sense of crisis',[39] which accounts for the tendency to overstatement and the recurring note of urgency in so many of his polemical writings. Here again, he was a man of his times, sharing with many of his contemporaries dark forebodings of imminent cataclysm. Opinions differed over the form that the blow might take: mob-violence leading to revolution, the consequence of failing to learn the lessons of what befell France in 1789; financial collapse like the disaster of December 1825, which demonstrated so painfully that fortunes easily made could be as easily lost. Such happenings fostered the spread of Millenarianism and expectations of Divine retribution for the sins of national wickedness.[40] Arnold was never a Millenarianist, but some of his language gives the hint of an approaching Armageddon. 'The Church as it now stands [in 1832], no human power can save'[41]; and, in a letter to Thomas Carlyle in 1840, 'I cannot, I am sure, be mistaken as to this, that the state of society in England at this moment was never yet paralleled in history.'[42] So, in his Inaugural Lecture at Oxford in the following year, he warned his audience: 'If there be any signs, however uncertain, that we are living in the latent period of the world's history… the importance of not wasting the time still left to us may well be called incalculable.'[43]

Arnold's first most controversial pamphlet on an ecclesiastical theme was his *Principles of Church Reform*, published in 1833, in which he declared his sincere conviction that the State and the National Church are really one and the same body, working for identical ends – the moral improvement of mankind. The major threat to the realisation of this ideal was sectarianism, and the worst manifestation of it in his own day was the concept of the Church as a clerical hierarchy, striving for uniformity of opinion and of worship, paying scant regard to the important role of the laity. Of course he had events in Oxford in mind. His proposed measures of radical reform filled almost all churchmen (and Dissenters) with horror – the sharing of church buildings by Christians of all denominations, who would hold their own services under their own chosen forms of worship at different times; doctrinal tests should be abolished; the order of deacons should be revived, tithes commuted, dioceses and parishes redistributed and the episcopal order thoroughly remodelled. Only by such sweeping reforms could unity be achieved. 'All societies of men, whether we call them states or churches', he wrote, 'should make their bond to consist in a common object and a common practice, rather than in a common belief; in other words, their end should be good rather than truth.'[44]

He seems to have known that he was pursuing a dream; but he observed, quoting a paradox of Hesiod, 'He is a fool who does not know how much the half is better than the whole.'[45] He hotly repudiated, however, imputations of unorthodoxy, claiming to be following in the line of Hooker, Burke and Coleridge. Certainly Coleridge had profoundly influenced Arnold's thought. 'I think with all his faults old Sam was more of a great man than anyone who has lived within the four seas in my memory',[46] he wrote in 1836. Arnold's affinity with what has come to be called the Broad Church tradition is even more clearly shown in his work on the 'Interpretation of Scripture'. He never doubted the inspiration of the biblical texts; what worried him was the way in which fundamentalists fought their corner. His professed aim was to place the Bible on 'an imperishable historical base that would be proof against any attack which the most refined modern learning could direct against it'.[47] This required, however, making concessions and admitting techniques of exegesis unpalatable to both Evangelicals and High Churchmen. The Old Testament, for instance, had to be read with an informed understanding of both the context of the events described and the moral code of the times in which they were written. All the scriptures should be scientifically studied on exactly the same methods and principles as one would employ in a study of the text of Thucydides.

Language, being a human instrument, must therefore be subjected to philological analysis.

If one aspired to rise to the rank of a 'sage' in early nineteenth-century England, there was one sure path to set you on your way: acquire a knowledge of German. This was how the Sage of Highgate (Coleridge) came to exercise the influence that he did; and this is what invested the Sage of Cheyne Row (Carlyle) with an aura of wisdom that his actual writings sometimes failed to confirm. Julius Hare – another Sage – directed Arnold along that same path in 1825, primarily to equip him with the resources to read Niebuhr. Arnold, therefore, was familiar with contemporary German critical scholarship, and it distressed him not a little to see how so many churchmen, for want of that knowledge, took 'alarm at the prevailing spirit' and were therefore afraid 'to yield even points they could not maintain, instead of wisely giving them up, and holding on where they could'.[48]

This was well and wisely said. Not so temperately expressed, nor so wise, however, was Arnold's attack on Newman and the Tractarians in his *Edinburgh Review* article of April 1836, to which the editor added the title 'The Oxford Malignants'. It was understandable, if barely excusable. Perhaps Arnold had never quite forgiven Newman for his off-the-cuff remark, 'But is Arnold a Christian?', on learning second-hand of the contents of the *Principles of Church Reform.* The chief reasons for Arnold's violent language, however, were twofold. He had been disgusted at the application by the Tractarians, in an improbable and short-lived alliance with the Evangelicals, of a sort of 'lynch law' aimed to embarrass and humiliate the allegedly heterodox Renn Dickson Hampden on his appointment to the Regius Professorship of Divinity at Oxford. Secondly, he firmly believed that Newman and his followers stood for everything most damaging to the health of the Church of England: on the one hand by their insistence on the centrality of dogma (to Arnold, Christianity was 'a life rather than a creed'), on the other by their sectarian spirit and their tendency to speak of the Church as if it were an exclusive clerical caste. As he expressed it to Edward Hawkins four years later: 'They have put a false Church in the place of the true, and through their counterfeit have destroyed the reality, as paper money drives away gold. And this false Church is the Priesthood, to which are ascribed all the powers really belonging to the true Church.'[49] He respected Roman Catholics as 'members of Christ's Church just as much as I am'.[50] Insofar as they stood as the enemies of Protestantism, they were 'a fair enemy'. The Newmanites, however, were 'a treacherous one'.[51]

Historians should be wary of predicting the future; and Arnold's forebodings were proved wrong. But his inclination, as we have seen, was towards the Cataclysmic; and he belonged to a school of historians – indeed, Duncan Forbes has cast him as the founder of them in this country[52] – who regarded the future with pessimism. These were the Liberal Anglican historians, who derived their inspiration from Niebuhr directly and also from their later study of Vico's *Scienza Nuova*: men such as Julius Hare, Dean Milman, Connop Thirlwall and, faithful disciple of Arnold to the last, A. P. Stanley himself. As a school, they rejected practically every production of recent and contemporary English historical study. Gibbon was anti-religious; Lingard was a romantic antiquarian; Macaulay believed too passionately in Progress, even to the extent of ultimate perfectability. Carlyle, however, shared their belief in the workings of Divine Providence throughout history, and Coleridge had instilled into them the importance of distinguishing 'cultivation' from 'civilisation'. Their pessimism, arising from a cyclical concept of history – civilisations rise only in time to fall – was strengthened by their contemplation of the potentially explosive social conditions of their own times, together with the perilously increased tempo of life within a society preoccupied with material conceits and industrialisation.

All these characteristics are found in Arnold's approach to history. There were lessons to be learned in abundance; not – curiously (for this was his blind spot) – from the 'noisome cavern' of the Middle Ages,[53] but most especially from the history of the ancient world, which demonstrated so many parallels with modern times that he completely rejected the traditional divisions of 'ancient' and 'modern'. Time and again, in his teaching of history at Rugby, he would ask his pupils 'What does this remind you of?'[54]

Arnold believed that all nations go through similar stages of development and that history is governed by law, just as in the world of nature. On the other hand, there are no timeless lessons to be learnt, and the historian must always proceed with caution and apply his critical judgment to safeguard against 'tearing examples out of context'.[55] The ability to draw analogies in order to read the signs and dangers of one's own times, however, was one of the historian's primary duties. This is why Arnold was so emphatic about the dangers of forcing the pace. One should not do so in the education of the young; similarly a nation must guard against forcing social or political changes too soon. Too much liberty all at once leads – he would say – to too much 'oxygen'.[56] Democracy will come, if it is to come, in its own good time.

Arnold's actual historical legacy was, through his early death, comparatively small. His *magnum opus* on the History of Rome reached no further than the end of the Second Punic War (three substantial volumes, nonetheless). He was full of plans for future projects on his appointment to the Oxford Chair and his later letters suggest that he had every intention of resigning the headmastership of Rugby once he had satisfied himself that he had enough funds to enable him to supplement the very meagre salary of a Regius Professor.

And so we must leave him, hoping that we have paid sufficient tribute to a complex character. He was an idealist, who had occasional flashes of discerning realism. 'It would give the vainest man alive a very fair notion of his own insufficiency', he once reflected, 'to see how little he can do, and how his most earnest addresses are as a cannon ball on a bolster.'[57] He was an autocrat who tended to distrust all authority except his own. He pined for the leisure to enable him fully to relax in his Lakeland retreat, 'Fox Howe', in Ambleside, but restlessness of disposition and his sense of mission would never really have allowed him to, much as he enjoyed the company of his family. He could at one moment cross playful spears with his pupils (not – I suspect – at Rugby) and, at another, cross angry swords with the leader of the Oxford Movement, in a sad conflict of mutual misunderstanding. He loved the study of the past, while always looking, usually with apprehension, at the present and the future. He composed pamphlets galore, many of them ephemeral, but also occasionally revealing that he was a man before his times. The word 'Man', he was wont to define in the following way: 'a being of large discourse, looking before and after'.[58] He might have been describing himself.

What might have been, had he been granted the normal span of years? This was the recurring question in the minds of his admirers. Charles Kingsley posed it, after reading Arnold's *Lectures on Modern History*. 'Oh why did that noblest of men die?', he mused in sorrow. 'God have mercy upon England! He takes the shining lights from us, for our National sin!'[59] Stanley reflected that 'What he actually achieved in his work falls so far short of what he intended to achieve, that it seems almost like an injustice to judge of his aims and views by them.'[60]

It is an interesting thought that had Arnold lived a little bit longer, Stanley would probably never have written his *Life*. The obvious author, according to the fashions of the time, would have been the most literary of Arnold's sons, Matthew, who in 1842 was just an undergraduate at Balliol, and a bit of a dandy as well; 'unmotivated' is the word we would use today; but, as his father put it, 'not apt to fix'.[61] What sort of book, I wonder, would have come from Matthew's pen?

It would certainly have been a tribute. In 1868, Matthew wrote to his mother as follows:

> The nearer I get to accomplishing the term of years which was papa's, the more I am struck with admiration at what he did in them. It is impossible to conceive him exactly as living now, amidst our present ideas, because these ideas he himself would have so much influenced had he been living the last twenty-five years, and, perhaps, have given in many respects a different course to.[62]

We shall allow Benjamin Jowett the final word. In 1878 he re-read Stanley's *Life* (apparently for the umpteenth time), and as was his oracular wont he sent his judgment to the author: 'There were weak points in Arnold and his friends intellectually, but in that one respect of inspiring others with ideals, there has been no one like him in modern times.'[63]

V

NEWMAN AND THE OXFORD MOVEMENT

This lecture was delivered at the National Portrait Gallery in the winter of 1968, as one of a series of six by different speakers under the general title of *The Victorian Crisis of Faith*. The lectures were subsequently published under this title by S.P.C.K. in 1970, edited by Anthony Symondson. I have made a few modifications to the original text.

V

NEWMAN AND THE OXFORD MOVEMENT

There can be no doubt whatever that the Oxford Movement was a response to a sense of crisis. 'The Church in danger' was its slogan. Horror at revolution over the water (the barricades were up again in Paris in 1830 and a French king set off disconsolately on his travels); fear of revolutionary elements at home; consciousness of change with the coming of the railways bringing with it the acceleration of society towards its possible doom; dismay at the dissolution of the Tory party over Catholic Emancipation and the rise of the Whigs to power, pledged to reform and prepared without scruple to ally with the forces of anti-clericalism in order to get their way: such were the tensions which drew churchmen of different traditions together, inspiring especially the younger and more fiery spirits among them to militant action, in a sure belief that a back-to-the-wall engagement would mark the 'Thermopylæ where the only effective stand should be made against the last inundations of lawless power'.[1]

In March 1829, John Henry Newman wrote to his mother from Oxford:

> We live in a novel era – one in which there is an advance towards universal education. Men have hitherto depended on others and especially the clergy for religious truth: now each man attempts to judge for himself ... All parties seem to acknowledge that the stream of opinion is setting against the Church.[2]

The sense of crisis gripped Oxford as it touched nowhere else. It was not only that Oxford was the traditional bastion of orthodoxy, or that, being the home of lost causes, it was likely to react dramatically to the threat of the imminent demise of the Church of England. More pertinent is the fact that Oxford during the late 1820s and early 1830s boasted amongst its senior members a number of energetic and unusually talented young men who all had these three attributes in common: an ardent pietism, derived on the whole from an Evangelical upbringing, an incomparable training in logic acquired through leading the field in the most formidably competitive test which the English academic world could offer, and finally a growing veneration for the teaching and example of John Keble. Furthermore, the furore over Catholic Emancipation in 1829 raged more vigorously and viciously in Oxford than anywhere else, and for good reason. Peel had committed a *volte face* and divided the Tory party; and Peel was member for the University. This was the issue which divided Oxford into rival factions and set the stage for the theological contests of the next decade.

For the next fifteen years Oxford was plunged into turmoil. Hardly for a moment did the sense of crisis relax. Mark Pattison, looking back on it all many years later, called it a nightmare.[3] Dean Church likened the atmosphere of the closely-knit and inward-looking University town to the storms which gripped the city-states of late medieval Italy: neighbour turning against neighbour, love and hate running to extremes.[4] Teachers and preachers whose disposition had marked them for a quiet life were thrust by a curious fortune into the role of party leaders, saluted as heroes or anathematised as blackguards, compelled to take sides on every political and theological issue of the hour. There was a universal consciousness of conflict and challenge, provoking great gestures and petty strife. We can sense the thrill of going into battle, when the first contributors to the *Tracts for the Times* marshalled their supporters and sent them riding off at break of day, satchels stuffed with tracts, to exhort the country clergy to magnify their office and to choose their side.[5] We can feel the tension in the Adam de Brome chapel at St Mary's, Oxford, as Newman unfolded in weekly instalments his *rationale* of the Anglican *via media*, his audience hanging on every word. Even the comic and the grotesque make a sort of sense in the heightened drama of these times: a Regius Professor deprived of his right to vote for select preachers because he had written a supposedly heretical book which few had read and nobody could understand;[6] dignified Heads of Houses and Doctors of Divinity hiding behind hedgerows to detect unwarrantable goings-on at Newman's supposed monastery at Littlemore;[7] and an eminent Headmaster of Rugby School slandered mercilessly because he had shown sympathy to dissenters and had allowed his pupils to discover that he had an eccentric and unconventional penchant for mixed bathing.[8]

What was it all about? It is matter of some doubt whether the principals themselves would have been able to give the same reply to that question. The answer hallowed by convention is that supplied by William Palmer, writing of the clamour for reform and the anti-clericalism of 1833.

> We knew not to what quarter to look for support. A Prelacy threatened, and apparently intimidated; a Government making its powers subservient to agitators who avowedly sought the destruction of the Church. The state, so long the guardian of that Church, now becoming its enemy and its tyrant. Enemies within the Church seeking the subversion of its essential characteristics and what was worst of all – no principle in the public mind to which we could appeal. [9]

In short, the enemies were Erastianism, in the sense of the claim by the state to dominate the Church, and latitudinarianism, by which was chiefly meant the weak churchmanship and liberal principles of Thomas Arnold. From the negative point of view, then, the Oxford cause was not a High Church attack upon the Evangelicals – why should it be? This was the religious tradition in which Newman himself had been nurtured and with him many of the principal adherents of Tractarianism. The pietistic element in Pusey was intensely strong, even if he was critical of Evangelical attitudes and acknowledged no such party affiliation.

The Evangelicals themselves were at one with the Tractarians in their opposition to Arnoldianism and Erastianism, and – because of the tensions within the party during the 1820s, especially on matters of Church order and religious decorum – were, in the persons of the wiser and worthier part at least, appreciative of the early efforts of the Oxford party to exalt the Church and defend ecclesiastical principles.[10]

It was not to be so for long, of course. And perhaps the sense of kinship was never more than superficial. The contrast is more clearly discerned when one turns to the positive aspects of the Oxford Movement. The clue to this is supplied by Henry Edward Manning in a letter written to Edward Coleridge in October 1845, shortly after the sad news of Newman's secession to Rome, although long anticipated, had been confirmed. Did this mean that the Movement had been a failure? Was all their work undone? No, answered Manning. The state of the Church, the changed atmosphere, the new consciousness of what a Church should be and of the truths to which the Church must bear witness, prove it not so. 'It is almost incredible', he wrote, 'that a body which fifteen years ago was elated at being an Establishment should now be conscious of being a Church.'[11] It was in the definition and elaboration of this ecclesiology, and the theological implications which followed therefrom – the exalted nature of the episcopate, the high sacramentalism, and especially the teaching on the nature of baptismal regeneration and the relationship of justification to sanctification – that the Evangelicals found themselves forced to part company from those who had seemed to be allies. And had they known more about the teaching of John Keble and the extent to which Keble had influenced Newman, they might well have drawn back from any expression of support from the beginning. This, however, requires a consideration of the respective attitudes of Keble and Newman, and an analysis of how these differences were reflected in their teaching.

John Henry Newman had a peculiarly receptive mind. It has often been observed of him that he had an uncanny knack, amounting almost to genius, of catching the spirit of a tradition, absorbing its ethos, and then – having partaken of such nourishment to his soul as the particular fount could supply – of imposing upon the teaching received his own distinctive interpretation; so that a mind which might at first appear to be that of an inspired eclectic reveals on closer inspection hidden depths of subtlety and originality, the stamp of the true philosopher who, while he learns from all who teach him, is never content with an interpretation which is not his own. This is why Newman, who was not the originator of the Oxford Movement, nor – at least in its early stages – its primary theologian,[12] was nevertheless the single genius which that movement threw up. John Keble inaugurated the movement and supplied the theological deposit, but it was Newman who gave it a perspective, who developed the original teaching into a distinctive ecclesiology, and who impressed his personality so deeply upon its concept of the religious life that Tractarianism could become more than an ephemeral manifestation of High Church pietism within the University of Oxford, but rather an enduring influence within the Anglican Church from 1830 to the present day.

Newman's was a restless mind, which always sought repose. In this he was utterly different from Keble. J.A. Froude has expressed the contrast thus:

> Newman's mind was worldwide. He was interested in everything that was going on in science, in politics, in literature. Nothing was too large for him, nothing too trivial, if it threw light upon the central question, what man really was, and what was his destiny ... Keble had looked into no lines of thought but his own. Newman had read omnivorously; he had studied modern thought and modern life in all its forms, and with all its many-coloured passions.[13]

The point should be taken further. All men have a certain number of natural or temperamental barriers, which effectively prevent particular ideas or trains of thought impinging powerfully upon their minds. A man who is tone-deaf (as Keble was, as a matter of interest) will never succumb to the blandishments of music because his ear is insensitive to pitch. Certain intellectual appeals likewise will cause but a jangle and a discord in a man's mind if his temperament prevents him from making any sort of sense of the premisses. We all possess what J. B. Mozley, writing of the illative sense in Newman's *Grammar of Assent*, describes as certain 'elementary convictions of the mind'[14] which determine our susceptibility to one argument and our incomprehension of another. Now Newman, receptive though he was, had such susceptibilities and mental blockages. He could not speak convincingly to an atheist, nor could he have been convinced by one.[15] It is doubtful whether he could have endured much converse with a liberal – by which he would mean a man who puts his faith in private judgment and who is therefore vulnerable to scepticism. For Newman, the dogmatic principle, the recognition of an ultimate and infallible authority, was one of those 'elementary convictions of the mind', induced by his conversion-experience at the age of fifteen and retained unshakably until the end of his life.[16]

Keble, by comparison, was a mass of these fundamental convictions. Whereas Newman went questing far and wide to find the dogmatic principle, Keble received it from his father and was satisfied. He imbibed the pure milk of the seventeenth century divines, and asked for no other fare, save that on which the Caroline divines themselves had fed: the Fathers. The tradition had been passed from country parsonage to country parsonage, and in such an environment, the slow-moving and insulated village of Fairford, Keble was left in his turn to guard the sacred deposit. He never went to school. He never, it seems, passed through a period of adolescence. As an undergraduate at Corpus he allowed no irreverent sally or dialectical engagement to ruffle his intellectual and spiritual composure. When rewarded with the highest academic prize that the University could offer – an Oriel Fellowship – he must have sat amidst the liveliest and sharpest minds in Oxford, feeling even as Newman did, and with less sound reason, *nunquam minus solus, quam cum solus*.[17] It was not that he was priggish: a humbler man never lived. It was just that he had ceased to be receptive, and so he stopped his ears. This parochial, self-contained character remained with Keble to the end. He went abroad but once; when tempted to take a break, he would make for the seaside seclusion of Torquay.

Keble, then, represents the static element in the Oxford Movement, although he was not so obviously static as the old 'High and Dry' Oxford Tories like William Palmer of Worcester College, with whom on occasion the Tractarians might seem to have walked in step. For Keble was, like Newman, a child of his times. Not even he could insulate himself against the prevailing mood of Romanticism, and indeed it penetrated to his very soul so that he put his theology into verse and became, without realising how exactly he had met the spirit of his time, the 'sweet singer in our Israel'.[18] In Keble, natural reticence and reverence subdue the passions and suppress exuberance, so that a poem is both an emotional experience and an intellectual challenge, the more emotional because of the sense of sobriety, the more intellectually alluring because of the appeal to the past rather than to the present – to a past captured not by colourful detail but by opaque imagery and recondite allusion, supplying ethos rather than fact.

Now Newman could have concourse with a mind like that, and could and did receive much. But there is a dynamism in Newman which meant that he could not stay with Keble for long. It was a dynamism very different from that of Hurrell Froude. Froude was all impetuous energy, an ardent crusader in need of a cause. Left to himself, Christopher Dawson tells us, 'Froude would have gone up like a rocket and left nothing behind him but a shower of sparks.'[19] He needed ballast – a steadying force, someone who could supply the cause and harness the energy. The coming-together of Keble and Froude in the Oxford reading-parties of the early 1820s was thus entirely felicitous to both men, for Keble could never have taken upon himself, without Froude's goading, the role of a militant in delivering the Oxford Assize Sermon of 1833 with its bellicose text: 'I will teach you the good and the right way'. After Froude's death in 1836 and the tragic change of direction which Newman appeared to be taking after 1841, Keble's brief period of active partisanship was over. As late as 1858 he had this interesting observation to make to Isaac Williams, thereby supplying the most revealing clue to his own role in the Oxford Movement that we possess:

> I look now upon my time with Newman and Pusey as a sort of parenthesis in my life; and I have now returned again to my old views such as I had before. At the time of the great Oxford Movement, when I used to go up to you at Oxford, Pusey and Newman were full of the wonderful progress and success of the movement – whereas I had always been taught that the truth must be unpopular and despised, and to make confession of it was all that one could do; but I see that I was fairly carried off my legs by the sanguine views they held, and the effects that were showing themselves in all quarters.[20]

The implications of this remark are very important indeed. To Keble the period when his teaching was taken up by younger men, developed and publicised in the *Tracts for the Times,* was really an irrelevance. He ought never to have allowed such a thing to happen; certainly he had failed in neglecting to dampen the ardour and banish the hopes of those who sought to proselytize his views. He would return to the peaceful contemplation of forgotten truths, in no way shaken by the fact that the episcopate had seemed to declare against them. Keble could stop his ears even to bishops. He would be a St Basil, declaring 'that God be true, though every man a liar'.[21]

It was because of his perception of this rock-like composure in Keble that Isaac Williams' account of the Oxford Movement in his *Autobiography* is so distinctive. It is the only history of Tractarianism that makes Keble the central figure. To Williams, who was always nearer to Keble than to Newman, the Oxford Movement had no inherent Romanizing tendency. No other substantial contributor to the *Tracts for the Times* felt the tensions that Newman was to feel. This was because there was always in Newman's allegiance to Tractarianism the desire to rove and to probe, which excited the occasional suspicion that he might only be a bird of passage. While Keble was content to demonstrate, Newman chose to put the Tractarian claims to the test. So it had ever been with Newman, and so it must always be. He knew where to seek the 'Notes of the Church'; felt in his bones, one might say (for Newman was a thorough Romantic), what the proper ethos must be: there must be a continuing tradition of saints and martyrs; there must be the sanctity of the first ages, the mark of the apostolate; somewhere on her body the Church must bear the stigmata of Christ. Of all the wise observations of his life-long friend R.W. Church, Dean of St Paul's, none was so penetrating as his final assessment of Newman's spiritual wanderings, which he offered in the *Guardian* shortly after Newman's death:

> Form after form was tried by him, the Christianity of Evangelicalism, the Christianity of Whately, the Christianity of Hawkins, the Christianity of Keble and Pusey; it was all very well, but it was not the Christianity of the New Testament and of the first ages. He wrote *The Church of the Fathers* to show they were not merely evidence of religion, but really living men; that they could and did live as they taught, and what was there like the New Testament or even the first ages now? Alas! There was nothing completely like them ... [22]

Later – years later – when the spiritual journeyings were over and Newman came to review his long but consistent investigations into the relationship between Faith and Reason in *The Grammar of Assent,* he saw the Odyssey that he had been through as something necessary and inevitable, a series of mental and spiritual exercises which mark the progress of the soul to Catholic truth. It conformed to what he came to describe as the *organum investigandi* given us for gaining religious truth, and which lead the mind by an infallible succession from the rejection of atheism to theism, and from theism to Christianity, and from Christianity to Evangelical Religion, and from these to Catholicity'[23] – a very teleological conception, we might say, as befitted an Oxford Aristotelian, but also a sentiment which betrays the conviction of the predestinarian, who knows that a hand is guiding him to the appointed end.

To Newman, then, the Oxford Movement was a phase in his spiritual progression; but he could not have so viewed it at the time, despite the suspicion of others; and the fact remains that during the time that he was the most active exponent of Tractarian teaching he contributed more to its theological insights than any other preacher or writer. Wherein, then, did Newman's originality lie?

His own answer was that he supplied little that was his own. Keble was the 'true and primary author' of the Oxford Movement.[24] Keble had the creative mind. This self-effacing assessment can be reasonably substantiated. In the main there were three leading ideas or lessons which Newman derived from Keble – an endearing respect, amounting to reverence, for the authority of the early Fathers; the consciousness of the true Catholic ethos, best conveyed by the medium of the doctrine of Reserve in Communicating Religious Knowledge; and finally, an understanding of the role of the Church and the sacraments, utterly different from what he had encountered in the teaching of either the Evangelicals or Richard Whately.

All three are of course related. In appreciating the one the enquiring mind will inevitably be led on to the others. But the Fathers come first. *In antiquis est scientia* – this was the first of Keble's lessons. One went back to the Caroline divines, to the continuators of the apostolic tradition who preserved the English Reformation from the errors of Continental Protestantism, and thence to the sources of their own inspiration, the Fathers themselves. What, in fact, did this mean? It brought one into a world of saints and martyrs, which had an instant appeal to the Romantic mind. It was not only that this world antedated the alleged corruptions of the Roman Communion – subservience to papal authority, mariolatry, invocation of saints, transubstantiation and the like – and therefore represented most faithfully the apostolicity, the spirit of primitive purity, which the Tractarians (they called themselves 'Apostolicals' as their chosen party label) sought to recover in the Church of their own day. It was the ethos of these times which touched the heart, having an epic, heroic quality – mighty deeds, self-sacrifice unto death, a sort of total theological involvement – which the Tractarians craved to emulate. Newman, Nicholas Wiseman, and Robert Wilberforce chose this setting for novels,[25] a setting which, one would have to admit, would seem from the point of view of the present day a little unpropitious. Much of this was Romantic idealism, but the intensity and desire to aspire to these heights was real enough. The celibacy cult of the Newman circle is the most obvious example of this. The nature of the times, and the state of the Church, demanded that a group of men should set such an example of self-sacrifice by deliberately choosing the celibate state, that 'high state of life', as Newman himself put it, 'to which the multitude of man cannot aspire'.[26]

All through his life, after his friendship with Keble began, Newman took the early Fathers as his primary source. His first published work was a history of the Arians,[27] followed by a series of articles on *The Church of the Fathers* published in the *British*

Magazine between 1833 and 1836. In the first of these articles, Newman stated his grand design to be to demonstrate 'the power of the Church at that time, and on what it was based, not (as Protestants imagine) on governments, or on human law, or on endowments, but on popular enthusiasm, on dogma, on hierarchical power, and on a supernatural Divine Presence'.[28] What it once was, so must it always strive to be. Such was the argument of the *Essay on Development*, Newman's gift to the Roman Catholic Church, a book as perplexing to his new co-religionists as it was to his old. The argument throughout is patristic, not Thomist or Tridentine; and he turned the tables on his Tractarian colleagues of old by arguing the Roman claims from the very sources which Anglicans were confidently using to repudiate them.[29] In his sermons, Newman constantly brought forward the patristic ideal:

> How unlike are the best among us to the Saints and Martyrs of old time; to St Cyprian, or St Basil, or St Ambrose, or St Leo! and what an utter mockery it is to couple their names with modern names, and to compare their words with our words, as is sometimes done! Yet, if true love be the tie that binds us to them, since they most certainly cannot move towards us, we through God's mercy perchance may be drawn to them.[30]

It is in *The Arians of the Fourth Century* that Newman developed most fully the second of the great truths which he derived from Keble, namely the doctrine of Reserve in Communicating Religious Knowledge, perhaps the most significant element in Tractarian teaching, for it takes us to the very bedrock of its theology and ecclesiology. Just as the appeal to the Fathers touched both heart and head, by evoking a sense of ethos and encouraging the study of dogma, so this particular tenet of patristic teaching contained implications both doctrinal and emotional. There is the doctrine itself, the *disciplina arcani,* most fully analysed from scriptural, patristic and more recent sources by Isaac Williams in Tracts 80 and 87; and the concept of the religious life which that doctrine implies, the form of religiosity which it engenders. Both aspects are of supreme importance for an understanding of the Oxford Movement.

The meaning of the doctrine is simply this: there is, as the Epistle to the Hebrews indicates, a distinction between the teaching which is appropriate for the weak and ignorant and that which is the property of a baptised and regenerate Christian. There are some to whom the mysteries must be told in parables; they need the 'nourishment of children rather than of grown men'.[31] In the words of Justin Martyr, 'knowledge is not safe without a true life'.[32] This was the assumption of the early catechetical schools and became the basis of Newman's own stated conviction that it was the role of the Church to teach, while appealing to Scripture as 'vindication of its teaching'.[33]

This was poles apart from the insights of Coleridge and Arnold in their exposition of the progressive nature of revelation, that as men grow through time and the accumulation of knowledge, so God reveals more of himself and his purposes.[34] The emphasis of Keble and Newman was on the need at any time for the Church to conceal or to disguise the sacred truths of which it was the guardian, to avoid pearls being cast before swine; and it was precisely this attitude of 'accommodation' – teaching by half-truths or appealing to superstitious and ignorant credulity – that Charles Kingsley attacked on the notorious occasion in 1864, when he accused Newman of teaching that 'truth is no virtue', thereby provoking perhaps the most celebrated riposte in the whole history of theological conflict.

To the Evangelicals, such teaching contradicted the fundamental article of their creed: the compulsion to preach the Gospel to every living creature; more than that, it denoted an attitude towards the religious life – a sobriety and secretiveness of disposition – which was the very antithesis of the accepted pattern of Evangelical behaviour and demeanour. A serious Christian was a man who wore his heart on his sleeve, who exuded Christian joy; like William Wilberforce, who seemed already in Heaven while on earth and who spoke of biblical figures and the saints as if he had known them personally as constant friends and companions.

Newman could never have been an Evangelical for long: the exuberance and religiosity were repugnant to him. In the first place, Evangelicals laid too great a stress on the role of feeling as a test of growth in grace, thereby betraying a naïve subjectivism in their understanding of religious experience. Secondly, the familiarity in their mode of address on things divine tended to cheapen and vulgarise sacred truths, especially in their histrionic sermons addressed to the masses, savouring of cant and blasphemy by the repetition of pious catchphrases and slogans supposedly for mutual edification. Newman tried to explain his distaste in a letter to James Stephen in 1835. He could not endure

> their rudeness, irreverence, and almost profaneness ... The poorest and humblest ought to shrink from the irreverence necessarily involved in pulpit addresses, which speak of the adorable works and sufferings of Christ with the familiarity and absence of awe with which we speak about our friends. Zaccheus did not intrude himself on our Lord – the woman that was a sinner silently bedewed his feet. Which of us is less refined than a 'tax-gatherer or a harlot?'[35]

Keble felt this too. The sobriety and austerity with which he dealt with holy things did not betoken a want of love. Far from it. The love that he bore was so precious that it was guarded and cherished in the utmost intimacy, never paraded or noised abroad. This explains his approach to poetry, which – to Keble – had almost a sacramental character: a means of conveying the most sacred truths by veiled allusions and subtle imagery, so that only those fit to receive them could fully understand.[36] So deeply did he feel this that he went so far as to defend the practice of the Professor of Poetry at Oxford lecturing in Latin on the esoteric nature of his art in order to ensure that the secrets were not divulged to the unworthy.[37]

I have dealt at some length with the doctrine of Reserve because, more than anything else, it explains the ethos of the Oxford Movement and the shaping of its ecclesiology and its sacramental theology. It is in this sphere that the originality of Newman himself primarily lies, and it constitutes his greatest individual contribution to the Oxford Movement. At a certain stage in the 1830s it might seem that the main focus of Newman's writings on ecclesiology was to demonstrate the Anglican Church's claim to be the *via media* between Roman corruptions and the heresies of popular Protestantism, but – as is well known – in the end he abandoned the attempt because he lost conviction in it. What he never lost, however, was his understanding of how the doctrine of Reserve could be translated into ecclesiological and sacramental terms, expressed most powerfully as early as May 1831 in his sermon on 'Christian Nobleness'.

'The Apostles' fellowship with Christ through the Spirit, after his ascension, was very different from their fellowship with him on earth', he writes. He then alludes to Christ's own words about the unforgivable sin of speaking against the Holy Ghost. He refers to St Paul: 'Work out your own salvation with fear and trembling'; 'Grieve not the Holy Spirit of God'. Then follows this great passage:

> This great truth is impressed upon the whole course of that sacred fellowship with Christ, which the Church provides for her children; in proportion as it is more high and gracious than that first intercourse which the Apostles enjoyed, so is it also more awful. When He had once ascended, henceforth for unstudied speech there were solemn rites; for familiar attendance there were mysterious ministerings; for questioning at will there was silent obedience; for sitting at table there was bowing in adoration; for eating and drinking there was fasting and watching. He who had taken his Lord and rebuked Him dared not speak to Him after His

> resurrection, when he saw and knew Him. He who had lain in His bosom at supper fell at His feet as dead. Such was the vision of the glorified Saviour of man, returning to His redeemed in the power of the spirit with a Presence more pervading because more intimate, and more real because more hidden. And as the manner of His coming was new, so was His gift. It was peace, but a new peace, 'not as the world giveth', not the exultation of the young, light-hearted and simple, easily created, easily lost; but a serious, sober, lasting comfort, full of reverence, deep in contemplation.[38]

The Church, then, is the medium for contact between finite and infinite. Where once the Lord had spoken to man in common speech, now – after the Redemption – the Spirit communicates through the sacraments. They are the prescribed channels: the joy of spontaneous communication is banished. In its stead must be the sobriety and reverence, which accompany the most solemn functions which the Church is empowered to perform – the safeguarding of the means of grace.

This was the message that came through time and time again in Newman's Anglican sermons, to read which brings one nearest to the heart of the Oxford Movement. The Church may represent the beauty of holiness. It was one of his major criticisms of the Church of his own day that it showed insufficient awareness of the yearning for Catholic externals, of the importance of satisfying 'the needs of the heart.[39] But above all it must inculcate the true apostolical ethos of severity.

> 'All is not gold that glitters' as the proverb goes; and all is not Catholic and Apostolic which effects what is high and beautiful and speaks to the imagination. Religion has two sides, a severe side, and a beautiful; and we shall be sure to swerve from the narrow way which leads to life, if we indulge ourselves in what is beautiful while we put aside what is severe.[40]

Now this is the point; and it is our final point. The way to life is 'narrow', even severe. The Church is not an Establishment, providing profession for 'smug parsons' with 'pony-carriages for their wives and daughters'.[41] This is what the Oxford Movement was chiefly about; and it was Newman's unique role to proclaim this particular message with an emotional power which none perhaps before or since has ever equalled. And herein, too, will be found the real reasons why Newman left the Church of his baptism at the cost of a broken heart. If his main contribution to the Oxford Movement had been to develop an ecclesiology, his translation 'to another portion of the Lord's vineyard' came about because he put that ecclesiology to the test. In the end he asked himself this question – which of the two Churches, the Anglican or the Roman, bore the enduring marks of the apostolic age, so that it would be immediately recognised as the true Church by one of the saints of old, should he be permitted to return to earth?

He put the position thus to one who was still wavering – A. J. Hanmer – in November 1849: 'To my mind the overbearingly convincing truth is this – that were St Athanasius or St Ambrose in London now, they would go to worship, not to St Paul's Cathedral, but to Warwick Street or Moor Fields. This my own reading of history has made to me an axiom, and it converted me, though of course I cannot communicate the force of it to another.' Newman must go to where the ethos of the fourth and fifth centuries is preserved still, where yet there remain 'altars, tombs, pilgrimages, processions, rites, relics, medals, &c. I hardly see a trace of the Church of the Fathers, as a living being, in the Anglican communion'.[42]

'Look on this picture and on that.' Looking to the Roman Church, Newman now recognised what he had sought – 'the movement of my spiritual mother *Incessu patuit Dea*'.[43] Not everyone would come to the same conclusion. It is an essentially subjective judgment. One looks for what one feels to have been the ethos of the Church of old, one tastes what the flavour of sanctity must have been. It is interesting and something of a paradox that, while Newman rejected Evangelicalism because it made feeling a test of growth in grace, he appears in the end to have accepted Romanism because he made feeling, above all else, the crucial test for discerning the identity of the one true Church. The Oxford Movement had been primarily a movement of the heart: Newman's conversion was as well.

VI

THREE BROTHERS: A.C., E.F. & R.H. BENSON

This paper was read to the E. F. Benson Society in London on 15 May 1986. It explores the relationship between the three Benson brothers (Arthur, Fred and Hugh), largely drawn from the extensive 180-volume diary of A. C. Benson, lodged in the library of Magdalene College, Cambridge.

VI

THREE BROTHERS: A.C., E.F. & R.H. BENSON

London, 15 May 1986

Few families have been so well chronicled as that of the Bensons. This fact is the more curious when one appreciates that their family history effectively spans only a single generation, beginning with the marriage of the young Edward White Benson to the even younger Mary Sidgwick in 1859, the year in which the couple took up residence at the newly-founded Wellington College in Berkshire, where in the course of Benson's fourteen-year spell as Master all six of their children were born. Two of the children died young: Martin, the eldest son, at the age of seventeen, and Nelly, the eldest daughter, at the age of twenty-seven. None of the remaining four (Arthur, Maggie, Fred and Hugh) married. There being no issue, therefore, there could be no continuing saga.

While one has to grant that Edward White Benson was an 'Eminent Victorian', sent by Disraeli to the new bishopric of Truro in 1877, and by Gladstone to the archbishopric of Canterbury in 1883, none of his children achieved comparable distinction. The brilliant Martin might have done so had he not fallen victim to meningitis while a Scholar of Winchester; so might Nelly, but for her early death from diphtheria. Maggie never really had a chance, either, suffering from chronic depression until she lost her reason completely in 1907. Of the remaining three boys, all became successful authors, although writing within a genre of differing degrees of ephemera. Hugh, the youngest, caused a mild sensation by taking Roman Catholic orders in 1903, and died eleven years later at the age of forty, having effectively burnt himself out in an orgy of militant proselytism, charted by the production of some twenty books of sentimental and dated Catholic apologetic.

Arthur and Fred Benson were even more prolific, their books equally reflective of the social circles in which they moved. Fred's circle was metropolitan – flashy, witty and moneyed – the world of the social climber and the *parvenu*, gossip in high places and not a little bitchiness, which Fred found the more fascinating because he had had to force himself into it and to learn its language. Arthur's circle was altogether more sedate and, arguably, a little more respectable – the world of the cathedral close, Eton, Cambridge and London-based literary friends. From an Eton housemastership, he became a Fellow and later Master of Magdalene College, Cambridge. He also became a very rich man, because the tone of urbane condescension in his books and the mild quietism of his philosophy, if such it can be called, found a ready market, especially among those who had no natural *entrée* into such privileged company and who felt flattered by his easy intimacies.

So two of the Benson children made fortunes for themselves and wrote, between them, nearly a hundred books. They had a famous father and a very remarkable, even adorable, mother. This might constitute a case for making the family worthy of study, but hardly answers the question – why do the Bensons command such an interest that of the making of books about them there would seem to be no end?

It must be significant that by far the majority of these books were written by themselves. Arthur and Fred between them contributed eight volumes of family reminiscence; and this is not to mention the many books of essays by Arthur which are either autobiographical or memoirs of members of the family and their friends. They were, then, as a family unusually self-absorbed, and admitted the fact. 'The Benson mind', Arthur once wrote, 'naturally thinks that anything which concerns itself is of the nature of a national crisis and a local convulsion. It is all lit up in a kind of golden glory, and the actors have tongues of fire on their heads.' They were, too, essentially a middle-class family that had risen above its natural station. Their grandfather, on their father's side, had been a practically penniless inventor who had blown himself up in a garden shed, which he used as a laboratory. Their father, however, became a member of the House of Lords, and – during his lifetime – the family lived in one or other of the archiepiscopal palaces at Lambeth and Addington. 'It is an interesting record intellectually', Arthur mused on this mid-nineteenth-century social phenomenon. 'Proctors, Bensons, Sidgwicks, Jacksons, but more intellectual than successful. We have got a middle-class taint about us. We are none of us aristocrats in any way'.

Their self-absorption had within it more than an element of self-justification. They were who they were because of what their father was or had been. They were proud of him, but also daunted. Martin and Nelly apart, the children feared him and avoided him, seeking always their mother's company. When Arthur came to write his father's biography, after his death in Hawarden parish church in 1896, he perceived the full tragedy of the situation. Their father genuinely loved his children, but found it impossible to express it except in occasional sentimental, even maudlin, touches. He could not relax with them, nor they with him. He could not resist the improving remark, while at the same time struggling with a sense of guilt that he had somehow brought about the early death of his eldest son by being over-exacting. There were moments when his hot temper, which had vitiated much of his good work at Wellington, would suddenly erupt. Fred for instance, never forgot a walk in Switzerland, on a family holiday, when Hugh was being unbearably provocative, and Fred had poked him with his umbrella. 'What did you do that for?', his father snapped. Foolishly, perhaps without thinking, Fred replied: 'Because I chose to.' The rejoinder was a sharp slap across the face from his father. 'I chose to do that', he said when he had delivered the blow. What a 'curious and sad story', Arthur wrote years later, when Fred told him about it.

The children felt guilty at their inability to show any love to their father, the more so when they came to realise, too late, how much he needed it. They felt, too, that they could never live up to his expectations. Arthur particularly was haunted all his life by the consciousness that he could never take the place of Martin who had promised so much. The relationship between these two older brothers had never actually been very close, especially after Martin had gone to Winchester and Arthur to Eton. 'He was very contemptuous ... of my want of knowledge, feeble memory, flaccid interest', Arthur recalled, 'and, at times, as if in a mood of regret, intensely affectionate, generally in absence. What a strange relation the relation of brothers is – a kind of compulsory friendship.' He couldn't compete; he didn't want to compete; but the sense that he was a disappointment to his father obsessed him. 'I had a good start in life', he reflected one day in 1909, when he was dining in Trinity College hall under the portraits of his father and of his uncle, Henry Sidgwick, 'I ought to have done better'.

Maggie's problems were intensified by a similar sense of guilt. She could not, temperamentally, take the place of Nelly, the only one of the six children who seemed to be able to be at ease with their father. At the same time she needed her father and deeply, if irrationally, resented his death coming when it did. Her sense of guilt was turned against her mother, expressing itself in fits of bitter antagonism when Mary Benson, as a widow, sought intimate companionship with Lucy Tait, the only surviving daughter of Benson's predecessor as Archbishop of Canterbury. Hugh was the only one of the six to take Orders (although Arthur had been expected to at any time during his twenty years as an Eton master), but the only way he could escape the shadow of his father's reputation and distinction was to minister within an alien Church.

Fred alone seemed to wear his sense of guilt most lightly, by deliberately cutting himself off from the ecclesiasticism and intellectualism of the family in order to live an independent life of his own within the London literary circle. All four of the children who survived into middle age seemed subconsciously to be saying in their different ways: 'we cannot compete in the arena in which we were expected to excel; we shall therefore be shamelessly self-indulgent'; only, of course, guilty feelings cannot be so easily eradicated as that. Betty Askwith puts it more strongly: the Benson children 'had so many gifts, but there is something twisted about them, something lacking, as if the pressure of their divinely endowed parents had been too much for them, as if they had never emerged from their adolescence, remaining on some deeper level, maimed and unfulfilled'.

This explains their enduring fascination and, indeed, their fascination for each other. They pursued different careers, but always the magnet of their family circle attracted them back, whether it was to enjoy the company of their mother or to feed upon their own self-absorption. To this extent they were a very close family and remained so throughout their lives. While their mother was alive (she died in 1918), they would return at regular intervals to Tremans, at Horsted Keynes, which became the family home in 1899. There they would often scrap and squabble and get on each other's nerves, but always there would be moments when they would close ranks and indulge in their particular family characteristics of exchanging witticisms about other people, seeking the right words to describe this or that idiosyncrasy of a friend, exercising a common talent for *voyeurism*, observing others, usually disrespectfully, and then setting the world (or more often the Church) to rights, without having to exert oneself to do anything active or positive about it. After a family gathering early in 1917, Arthur wrote in his diary:

> What is wrong with us as a family is that we are *performers* essentially. Fred told me the other day that he got an anonymous letter from a woman – 'Why aren't you in khaki? No Benson ever did anything for anyone else.' I think this is decidedly true. We are

individualists and require both money and applause. No interest in the lost sheep of the House of Israel.

The self-absorption became, then, a sort of self-indulgence. This may account for certain other attributes of the family, which they possessed more or less in common. Introversion and a lurking sense of guilt are all hallmarks of the depressive. Their father had been a manic depressive, his moods switching from high elation and intense activity to black moments of crippling despair. Hugh's restless and perverse vitality undoubtedly sometimes concealed a deep inner unhappiness and insecurity. Maggie lost her reason entirely in 1907, never to recover. Arthur, who had two periods of complete breakdown during his life when he wrestled with 'the wild beast beside me', believed that he was a victim of some inherited malady and that the whole strain might be tainted with incipient insanity; one reason – he suggested – why they had a duty not to marry and to perpetuate the line. Fred, however, seems to have been spared this particular anguish, unless what Arthur was wont to describe as his 'breezy materialism' was sometimes only a rather aggressive veneer. 'His cheerfulness does not lie very deep', Arthur wrote in 1909. 'His subconscious is an irritable and easily-bored thing', adding, singularly inappropriately, 'while mine is placid and contented'.

Arthur did, however, concede that Fred was the only member of the family who might seriously contemplate marriage. 'Fred understands women', he said in 1898, 'while I don't. They seem to me too high-minded and not so much unselfish as desiring to be held so. I don't understand their absence of logic, their quick transitions, their prejudices, their need to be caressed mentally, their need to triumph in small ways, their adroitness of management.' A year later, he wrote in his diary: 'I implored Fred to marry. He is the only one of us likely to. We are the only Bensons of our line left.'

Not that Arthur approved at all of the sort of women that Fred liked to count among his circle, with the single exception of Lady Evelyn Lister who was a frequent visitor to Fred's house in Audley Street during 1908. But nothing came of that as Fred, thereafter tended to succumb to the lure of sentimental male friendships – a whole succession of 'mysterious young friends', Arthur commented, while admitting that, in his own case this was a form of self-indulgence, giving him aesthetic pleasure without imposing the slightest demand or obligation upon himself.

The third attribute which the Bensons had in common was their sense of humour: irreverent, delighting in the incongruous, the grotesque and the absurd. On a walk in 1911 with Gertrude Bell, while Arthur was visiting Sir Hugh Bell at Rownton in Yorkshire, the physiognomy of the Welsh came up in conversation. Arthur pronounced them as a race 'ugly… with faces like goats and parrots seen in spoons'. 'There', said Gertrude Bell, 'that is a characteristic Benson remark. I like getting in touch with that again … You are not in the least like the children of Archbishops.' Perhaps not; although there is a touch of humour of the children of the manse in Fred Benson's coming-down to breakfast at Tremans, bawbling:

> Dark and cheerless is the morn
> Unaccompanied by tea

Or – even more typical – Fred's delight in recounting an episode at the funeral of the baby of their mutual friend, Robin Strutt:

> The sentimental parson said to Willy Strutt, 'But after all it is a joy to think of the dear child, is it not, as clasped safe in the bosom of Jesus?' 'Ripping', said Willy, with a perfectly inexpressive face and an eye like that of a goat.

They liked poking fun at clerical friends. The Creightons were always fair game, because of the pompous pleasure of Mrs Creighton at becoming a bishop's wife: a vein of unpleasing self-satisfaction, which had infected all the family. Mary Benson told the assembled company at Tremans about Oswyn Creighton's first sermon after he had been ordained deacon. 'No praise, please', he had said to his Rector, as he called in at his study after the service. The Rector looked at him severely. 'I am afraid I had not intended to praise it. I was going to ask you to count and see how many times the pronoun "I" occurred in it.'

Anything with a touch of the incongruous appealed to them. They liked playing, after dinner, a game of consequences called 'Heads, Bodies and Legs', making grotesque figures out of cards. There was an acting game, when the others had to guess pairs of improbable characters, the pairing of Queen Victoria with Cleopatra arising from the story of the old lady who, having been to the theatre to see *Antony and Cleopatra*, had declared that it 'was very fine; but a painful contrast to the home life of our own dear Queen'.

On the other hand, these occasions when the family assembled at Tremans could produce their irritations. The problem was that each of the three brothers were bachelors, living their independent and very different lives, cherishing their own self-chosen routine. Inevitably when they lived together under the same roof, with their mother as hostess, their determined efforts to preserve the sacrosanctity of their own routine threatened to impinge upon the convenience of others. Arthur liked to sit in bed over his morning tea, reading. But Hugh had converted a room next door into a little oratory in which he would say Mass each morning, and would distract Arthur with his indistinct mumblings and the occasional tinkling of the sacring bell. Fred would infuriate Arthur and Hugh by sulking when they embarked upon a theological discussion and would go over to the piano and indulge in loud, coarse strumming, or – rather more ambitiously, though no less irritatingly – plough an uneven and unsteady passage through a Handel fugue. If the others wanted to go for a walk, Fred would either be obstinate and refuse to stir, or he would walk at a pace too fast to allow Arthur to muse on the beauties of the countryside. They were none of them good losers at cards. On one occasion, during a game of Jacobi, Fred became so exasperated over his lack of success that he snapped at Arthur, 'Don't talk so much!'

All of this suggests, of course, that they were really very alike, these three brothers; especially in their faults. These were scrupulously chronicled in Arthur's diaries, not as evidence of any ill-will towards them, but quite the reverse. The closer one was to Arthur the more readily he would portray his friends and companions warts-and-all. Nor, indeed, did he write in any spirit of self-righteousness, because he was honest enough to recognise that the faults one perceives in others are almost always the very faults that they perceive in you.

He could be scathing at times in writing about Hugh, more so than anything he could find to condemn in Fred. Yet the bond between Arthur and Hugh was very close and mutually acknowledged. They quarrelled fiercely, usually on theological issues. Arthur hated any sort of dogmatism, any claim on the part of another to be in the possession of absolute truth. Hugh revelled in all those aspects of Roman Catholicism that Arthur disliked most: its claim to infallibility, its love of ritual, its exploitation of the credulous. Arthur knew, too, that there was an element in Hugh whereby – true to his provocative and Puckish nature – 'he only does it to annoy because he knows it teases'. This was Hugh all over: the love of being outrageously perverse, of making a virtue of his defects and vices, of being thoroughly selfish when it suited him. Nevertheless Arthur was always temperamentally nearer to Hugh than to Fred. Whenever Arthur and Hugh were together, Fred felt excluded. He hated talking about religion in any serious vein, for instance. As Arthur put it, writing in 1909, 'he seems to accept all the cardinal doctrines (of Christianity) as a child of eight would'. He constantly shied away from anything too personal. There was an awful occasion, shortly after his father's death, and the family were living in Winchester, when they received a visit from John Reeve, Vicar of Addington, a man of corrigible earnestness who had known all the family as children at Truro. He turned to Fred in front of the others and asked him, to his intense embarrassment and to the barely-concealed delight of the rest of the family, whether he prayed for the repose of Mr Gladstone's soul. Hugh, in certain moods, had the same effect upon him. 'Hugh gets on his nerves', Arthur recorded, after all three had been together at Tremans early in 1908. 'Indeed we all do, I think. It is quite curious to see how it affects his very looks. When he is out walking and cheerful, he is the picture of health and bonhomie. When he argues with Hugh, he becomes wrinkled and even ugly with a sort of dusky look.'

The trouble with Fred, Arthur believed, was that he could not bear to be serious. Indeed, his advancement through life seemed to contradict the normal progression. In 1910, Arthur reflected: 'Fred is a curious creature. Now 43, with the inactivity in almost everything of a boy. It is so odd that he was such an old grandpa when he was a child and now such a child when he begins to be grey-headed.'

It was not surprising really. Fred quite self-consciously turned his back on the life of the cathedral close when he came down from Cambridge. His whole circle of friends was to be different, and he felt out of his element when he returned to Tremans. They could not really understand his world and he was bored by the seeming pettiness of their own concerns. Why should Arthur get so pompous about a disciplinary decision that he had to take over the young Duke of Albany, a boy in his house at Eton? What did it matter? Arthur rebuked him stiffly for calling his professionalism into question. This was in 1899, and occasioned a savage comment in Arthur's diary, deploring 'the provincial atmosphere' of Fred's life: golf in the daytime, then cards at the Club in the evening. 'Fred begins to remind me of the heroes of Mrs Oliphant's books, drawn from her own unhappy son.' Then later: 'I don't like the people Fred goes with. I mistrust them all.'

This was a recurring complaint. It put Fred on the defensive and he therefore began to name-drop. In return, Arthur was contemptuous about this 'curious world of dim aristocrats' which Fred was so keen to talk airily about, making his visits to any member of the family seem as if 'he were a great man visiting an almshouse'. Actually he believed that Fred's horizon was getting steadily narrower, while he himself 'has serene consciousness of being in the swim, because he goes to stay with absurd countesses like Lady Radnor, whose vagaries I cannot think that he would tolerate if she was Mrs Tompkinson'. He listened with amazement to Fred expounding his theory that the English people were not, as a race, snobbish, not caring tuppence whether their friends were Dukes, Marquesses, or whatever. How could a man be so deluded, Arthur thought, as he wrote up his diary that night? 'I think [people] care a great deal; and may God forgive me, but I am sure Fred does.' On one occasion in 1911, when all the family were assembled at Tremans, the conversation turned – characteristically – to the Psalms. Arthur noted Fred's contribution to this – for him – unpropitious subject:

> His only interest in the psalms seemed to be that Lady Balfour of Burleigh knew so many of them by heart. M.B. [their mother] said that she loved Psalm 119 and I agreed, but Fred cried that Lady B of B didn't know it – only a few bits here and there.

By 1910, Arthur began to worry whether this flashy, moneyed set into which Fred had gained an *entrée* might prove his undoing in some unhealthy and undefined way. He had been talking with Percy Lubbock who had given him a rather disturbing picture of the mode of life of some of Fred's friends in the English quarter in Venice:

> Charles Williamson in his Palazzo, Lady Radnor in her saloons – the silliness of it, the idleness, the sentimentality about bronzed gondoliers &c, with I dare say a nastier background, was all very interesting. It is this life which Fred leads so mysteriously and of which he says nothing. I wonder what it is all about.

Later that year, Fred, having now set up house in Cromer, came to stay at Tremans and horrified Arthur still further. 'He was full of the charms of *simplicity*, and of simple people, by whom I fear he means wealthy and ennobled Jews who are frankly vulgar.' After a further eulogy from Fred about 'that dear old goose, Lady Radnor', he and Hugh pooled their thoughts about Fred's naivety.

> We are both rather in terror of what he may become – a jawing Major of the Smoking Room. His stories become more stereotyped, the people he knows fewer and more Semitic; and he is so pleased with himself and his work and his little bits of silver and his friends and everything.

He felt, after talking with Hugh so frankly, that he had discovered the essence of the difference between his two brothers and why he so much preferred Hugh's company to Fred's. 'You may say things, involving ideas, to Hugh. He may not agree, but he will understand, and he will disagree because he thinks differently. Fred will not understand, and will disagree because he does not understand.'

Was he a little jealous of Fred's success? He admitted Fred's 'cleverness' but thought both his characterisation and philosophy shallow. 'No one in any of Fred's books', he wrote in 1914, after reading *Dodo II*, 'ever seems to have had to do anything that he or she didn't like – and they are supposed to atone for all their prattling and fooling by a flash of courage or emotion.' It pleased him rather that when he went to see the stage version of the original *Dodo*; it was billed together with a one-act play by Bernard Shaw. Shaw was sitting in a box, looking on with smiles. The two plays, Arthur thought, 'revealed the differences between an amateur and a pro'. As for *David Blaise*, Arthur dismissed it as 'conventional and, in a curious way, priggish….He touches on delicate questions rather crudely…It either ought to be handled as a problem or else skated over'.

Perhaps this comes rather ill from somebody whose own books are hardly memorable for their profundity. The truth is, however, that Arthur could never take Fred seriously. Fred thrived on gossip; his inaccuracy, arising from his delight in improving a story, was notorious. He was only too ready to pronounce on politics, but what did his politics amount to? Just 'scraps of Tory gossip, imperfectly remembered'. Arthur was at his most snappish with Fred during the early years of the war, after a particularly harrowing Christmas at Tremans in 1915, when Fred was full of inside information about doings at the Front, gathered – as Arthur cuttingly put it – 'from mysterious unnamed people, in high official position, who only confide in Fred'.

For all this mixture of mockery and pique, Arthur recognised one particular quality in Fred, which was conspicuously absent in Hugh. If ever in trouble, if he needed help in any tangible form, Fred would be the one who would come to the rescue, not Hugh. Despite his soft and boyish looks and the unashamed sentimentality of his books, Hugh guarded his independence with a selfishness that bordered on hardness. When Maggie needed funds to pay for her treatment at a private clinic, Fred and Arthur willingly contributed. Not so Hugh. He was dismissive and would not pay a penny. 'Back to the Priory' (the mental hospital at Roehampton) was his response. During Arthur's first mental breakdown, between 1905 and 1907, it was Fred, time and again, who cancelled his engagements in order to try to help him through. Arthur knew this, and – at the time – was almost pathetically grateful. Often enough, however, it was the gratitude of the valetudinarian, which could easily turn to a sort of resentment against the aggressive good health of his helpmate. Fred took not the slightest care of his own constitution, Arthur would complain, drinking far too much whisky (for instance) – he noted in 1907 – at lunch, tea and dinner. It seemed hardly fair. While Fred seemed to admit 'no failure or despondency … I come to the melancholy conclusion that I have been living too inactive and contemplative a life with my mind turned in upon itself'. He had adopted the style of life of a man of sixty when he was only 45.

Fred didn't know what it was like to be ill, Arthur selfishly reflected. When in 1909 Fred was laid low by something called a 'streptococcus', he made himself pathetically absurd by assuming a sort of 'deathbed voice'. All he could show for his ailments was 'a small red pimple perhaps the size of half a dried pea'. He was a little more sympathetic in April 1913, however, when Fred was suffering from a swollen kidney, brought on – Arthur noted with a sort of self-righteous satisfaction – from drinking too much fluid in the evenings. He visited the invalid at his home in Ockley Street, finding him lying miserably on a sofa, forbidden either to smoke or to drink. A kidney was eventually removed, and Arthur reciprocated Fred's solicitousness by visiting him after the operation, noting that although he was obliged to give up drinking whisky, he seemed happy enough sitting up smoking in bed.

It was not really until Arthur's longer and more serious mental breakdown, between 1917 and 1923, that he fully conceded how much he had come to depend upon Fred. Hugh had died (in 1914); Maggie's death, a merciful release, had followed in 1916. Then, during Arthur's long incarceration in the nursing-home at St Michael's, Ascot, Mary Benson – the anchor of the whole family – herself died in 1918. Arthur was too ill to attend her funeral. Of the Benson family, only Fred and Arthur remained.

Inevitably, then, they were thrown together, because Arthur, when discharged from St Michael's, could not be left alone. Sometimes Percy Lubbock, occasionally David Loveday, but more usually Fred looked after him. In the late summer of 1922 they set up house together, for a short while, at Blakeney on the Norfolk coast. It was not an easy time. Fred had become very rheumatic, but was still in high spirit. Arthur refused to concede that actually the clouds of his depression were slightly lifting. They took daily walks along the sea wall; each evening they played chess, Arthur usually losing. Fred gradually nursed him back to receiving social calls, calming the panic that would rise in Arthur at the prospect of having to seem cheerful and to adopt company manners.

It was slow progress. During the latter part of 1922, the scene changed to Rye, to Lamb House where Henry James had lived, Fred having secured it on a tenancy for a part of each year. They spent Christmas together there. 'I felt it sad', Arthur wrote, 'that the old family life had come down to this, two moderately successful men – no children; Fred in much discomfort [from rheumatism] and I in the nethermost pit.' Then, one evening in the spring of 1923, it occurred to Arthur that – after being beaten at chess for the umpteenth time – he no longer felt annoyed or crushed. The clouds had suddenly lifted. Thereafter, until his sudden death from a heart attack, back in the Master's Lodge at Magdalene, in June 1925, he was his old self again. It was Fred who was more of the invalid now – 'very lame and stiff, thighs much shrunken' Arthur observed. 'He swallows strange decoctions and applies unpleasant douches. 'While he was supposed to submit to a strict diet, this was honoured more in the breach than in the observance. 'Just as a treat', he would say, as he produced some forbidden delicacy or helped himself to another drink.

These perhaps were the twilight years; happy ones, nonetheless. At last they began to respect each other's way of life. While Arthur was entertaining his young Cambridge friends – George (Dadie) Rylands, Bernard Lord Manning, Sebastian

Sprott, Noel Blakiston – Fred would disappear for a spell at Bath with the eighty-year-old (and now enormously stout) Lady Radnor, or go to his town house in Brompton Square. When they were together they talked more frankly to each other than they had ever done before. They discussed their parents, having both read Mary Benson's private diary. Arthur commented:

> It seems to me that they were two very vivid and splendid people, but utterly antagonistic in temperament, and probably ought never to have married ... We wondered if they had ever *really* loved. Certainly I never remember them seeking each other's company or wanting to be alone together.

They also talked about their male friendships. With both of them, as with Hugh and indeed with so many of their respective circles, all the deepest emotional passions that they had felt had been directed towards young men or to like-minded men friends. Arthur's whole life had been punctuated with little sentimental romances – some, as with Eton boys like Percy Lubbock, Julian Grenfell and Edward Horner – at a discreet and dignified distance; others – as with George Mallory, Geoffrey Winterbottom, Geoffrey Madan and Dadie Rylands – at a rather more passionate level, but nonetheless chaste. At the time that they discussed the phenomenon, a new little romance was just beginning, in Arthur's fancy, with the young Noel Blakiston. The only relationship that had gone distinctly sour, because of the intensity of his partner to express the bond in a more overtly sexual form, had been his friendship with Hugh Walpole. What Arthur wrote of his brother Hugh, however, was largely true of himself. 'He never had the slightest touch of sexual passion. He liked friends and he loved children, but he shrank from women.'

Fred's romantic liaisons with certain 'mysterious young friends' (as Arthur called them) were probably of the same nature; as his relationship with Philip Burne-Jones, Frances Yeats Brown and John Ellingham Brooks ('a fallen English country gentlemen', as Arthur described him on hearing of their setting-up house together in Capri in 1913) may have been no more overtly sexual than Arthur's enduring friendship with the effete Howard Sturgis or Percy Lubbock's infatuation for the young painter, Adrian Graham. It all depends on what one means by homosexuality. When Arthur and Fred discussed the meaning of this word one evening in April 1924, it is clear that it was reasonably new to their vocabulary. While it never occurred to them to apply the term to themselves, for neither they nor their contemporaries regarded intense emotional attachment between people of the same sex as necessarily unhealthy, they came to the conclusion that the ethical standards of the day were curiously awry 'if marriage should be a sort of virtuous duty, honourable, beautiful and praiseworthy, but that all irregular sexual experiences should be bestial and unmentionable'. The real test should surely be 'the concurrence of the soul'. Theoretically, they had no abhorrence of a physical liaison between people of the same sex, if the depth of the mutual love led naturally to that form of expression. But in actual fact Arthur himself was psychologically inhibited from ever allowing such a thing to happen. Sometimes he rather regretted it, suspecting that this arose from timidity as opposed to moral conviction; but there it was. This was the frankest discussion that he and Fred had ever had. Returning to Cambridge the next day, Arthur wrote in his diary: 'I was sorry to go. I have never found Fred in such a wholly gentle and sympathetic mood.'

The last summer that Arthur spent at Lamb House was, indeed, a happy one – 'the garden full of roses and flowers, most lovely. The tortoise was eating marigolds with a jocose air, blank fixed eyes, and sucking the stalks. Twenty times he would bite at a leaf and twenty times miss it': a very typical vignette. On the occasions that he and Fred were together, they were – in Arthur's words – the 'two hobblers', as they made their sedate progress through Rye. Pass a year, however, and Arthur was dead. It was left to Fred to determine his memorial.

It was a happy inspiration to combine with Madame de Nottbech, Arthur's American admirer and munificent benefactress, to commission a memorial window in Rye parish church. In every sense it was appropriate. Arthur delighted in stained glass, chiefly because it gave such scope for amusement over the incongruities wrought by the lack of perspective; and there he is himself in the bottom right hand panel, unmistakeable in the likeness. Magdalene College is there, too, in the background, redolent of *From a College Window*, the book that established Arthur's fame as an essayist. The Master of Magdalene is portrayed as a kneeling figure, surveying piously an open book, with the words 'Thy Rod and Thy Staff' (another best-seller) in such huge letters that they fill both pages. Most exquisite of all, Arthur Benson is draped in his scarlet LLD gown. Fred knew how much he valued this accolade, granted to him *jure dignitatis* when he became Master of Magdalene.

How would Arthur have memorialised Fred if he had been the one to be left? He would have found something appropriate, I have no doubt. It would have been a statue, I fancy; a solitary statue seen at the end of a long avenue (one of Arthur's favourite vistas); probably a bulky statue with a stick. One thing is sure, however. He would not have put him in stained glass.

VII

HOW SOAPY WAS SAM?: A STUDY OF SAMUEL WILBERFORCE

This article was published in *History Today*, volume XIII, number 9, in September 1963. I have made a very few alterations to the original text.

VII

HOW SOAPY WAS SAM?: A STUDY OF SAMUEL WILBERFORCE

On a hot summer's evening in mid-July 1873, the Bishop of Winchester was thrown from his horse while riding with Lord Granville. He had just been commenting on the beauty of the trees and the excellence of his mount; a moment later he was dead. Thus Samuel Wilberforce's career was cut short while he was still at the height of his powers, and – in the words of R. W. Church (whose judgments posterity has tended to endorse) – the Church of England lost her 'greatest bishop … for a century and a half'.[1]

Dean Church's words are startling if only because so little of Wilberforce's life and work has survived in popular memory. We recall a name – 'soapy Sam' – and a *faux pas* involving T. H. Huxley, but very little else: a pathetic residuum of an active life, the details of which rarely escaped public notice. Indeed, the eyes of the world had been fastened upon all the Wilberforce children since their infancy. After all, their father, who had gained in his own lifetime recognition as a saint, had publicly renounced his position as MP for Yorkshire in order to devote more time to their education and religious training; and the atmosphere of deep piety and Christian joyousness which pervaded the Wilberforce family circle seemed to represent the perfection of an Evangelical upbringing and rapidly became the model of Victorian family life. Great things were expected of William's sons; although he himself wished no more than that they should become pious and useful clergymen.

His eldest son (William) went grievously astray while his father was still alive, dissipating the bulk of the Wilberforce fortune. His other three sons (Robert, Samuel and Henry) promised better. By the time of William's death in 1833 they had all gained firsts at Oriel College, Oxford, Robert and Samuel had taken Anglican orders and Henry was preparing to do the same. No one could have foreseen the sorrows that were to come. Henry, brilliant and impulsive, became the ardent disciple of Newman and was received into the Roman Church in 1850; and Robert, the most scholarly and retiring, followed his example four years later, mainly through the influence of Henry Edward Manning. There remained only Sam to fulfil the aspirations of his father and to maintain the connection between the family name and devoted service to the Church of England.

That he succeeded in doing so none would deny. His rise to high office within the Church was meteoric. Ordained to a curacy at Checkenden, near Henley in 1829, he became Rector of Brighstone on the Isle of Wight a year later, at the age of twenty-four. By the time he was forty he had been elevated to the bishopric of Oxford, having gained in rapid succession the offices of rural dean, Archdeacon of Surrey, Canon of Winchester, Sub-Almoner to the Queen and Dean of Westminster. During the same period he passed from the Evangelicalism inherited from his father, and reinforced by his marriage to the eldest surviving daughter of John Sargent, the beloved friend of Charles Simeon and Henry Martyn, into the ranks of the moderate High Churchmen in the company of his brother Robert and his brother-in-law Henry Edward Manning.

It was clear that the move to Oxford would make or break him. The diocese had recently been enlarged by the addition of the counties of Berkshire and Buckingham, and the University itself was reeling under the blow of Newman's secession to the Roman Church. Wilberforce's task was to restore peace while harnessing to the service of the Establishment the zeal and spiritual vitality which had led to religious war. As events turned out, the Oxford episcopate *did* break him – in one sense at least – for early misfortunes were to lose him the favour of the Court and to delay preferment for twenty-four years. Although his public reputation was immense, as the leading spirit in the revival of Convocation in the 1850s, the champion of orthodoxy in his attacks upon *Essays and Reviews*, Bishop Colenso and Darwin's *Origin of Species*, and as one of the chief ecclesiastical spokesmen in the House of Lords, he was repeatedly passed over for further office until Gladstone paid the debt of old friendship and enduring admiration by recommending him for the bishopric of Winchester in 1869.

On the other hand, the thwarting of his personal ambition to become Primate proved in the long run a blessing. For the significance of the work of Samuel Wilberforce in the history of the Anglican Church lies neither in his role as a great ecclesiastical statesman nor in the prestige which he enjoyed among his episcopal brethren, but rather in the less conspicuous triumphs of his diocesan administration and pastoral influence. Wilberforce not only brought peace to his troubled diocese, but – in the example he set of indefatigable pastoral zeal, whether through diocesan missions or through the personal contact that he always maintained with his clergy and with the ordinands at Cuddesdon, the theological college which he founded in 1854 – he created a new model of the office of a bishop within the Anglican Church. This was the judgment of his fellow-churchmen like Dean Burgon, Christopher Wordsworth, R. W. Church and William Palmer, who came to see in Wilberforce's work the true fulfilment of Newman's labours for the Church of England.

> When Newman abandoned his work in despair [wrote William Palmer in 1833], others stepped in to complete and expand it ... A more practical and beneficial agency arose, which taking what was good and true in Newman's system, and accordant with the Church of England, placed these principles in a higher and nobler and more practical attitude. As it was said of Saul, 'He hath slain his thousands', but David his 'tens of thousands', so it was in this case. Newman laid the foundations, but Wilberforce built up the temple.[2]

In recent years this view has been confirmed by Dr Ronald Pugh; and to his conclusions may be added the opinion of the Swedish scholar, Dr Yngve Brilioth, who has described Wilberforce's achievement as uniting Evangelicalism and Tractarianism 'into a new and living synthesis', thereby inaugurating a new type of High Churchmanship.[3]

Samuel Wilberforce's popular memorial, however, has been somewhat less respectful; and it may profit us to consider why this is so. Most particularly, how did he acquire the notorious epithet of 'soapy', which, when applied to the diminutive of his Christian name, was found to be so euphoniously satisfying and maliciously apt?

The publication of the official *Life of Samuel Wilberforce* in three volumes, the first written by A. R. Ashwell in 1880 and the two succeeding volumes by the Bishop's eldest surviving son, Reginald Wilberforce in 1881-2, provoked a storm of controversy in the Press, which reached its climax in December 1882 when the reviewers were first confronted with the competed work. It was considered sensational in its revelations. R. G. Wilberforce had been especially indiscreet, quoting large portions of his father's diaries – acrimonious comments about his opponents, accounts of private conversations and unauthenticated anecdotes about eminent persons still living regardless both of the supposed wishes of the late Bishop himself and of the susceptibilities of those whom he so bitterly attacked. Those who were astounded and enraged at the contrast between Wilberforce's charm and courtesy in public and the malevolence of his inner thoughts were not slow to revive earlier charges of insincerity, duplicity and time-serving against 'soapy Sam', and were scarcely appeased by R. G. Wilberforce's reply that 'could you see the materials which I have not yet published, you might marvel at its [the book's] amazing moderation!'[4]

In the columns of *The Times* during January 1883 the amateur phrase-hunters set to work, propounding various theories as to the origin of the sobriquet which recent controversy had made topical. First came 'W.H.T.', on 2 January, with an explanation allegedly from the lips of Robert Wilberforce himself, who – having heard two neighbours discussing his brother's popular title in the gallery of the House of Lords sometime in 1849 or 1850 – interrupted their conversation by pointing out that 'soapy Sam' was a domestic nickname arising from the fact that 'as a boy he was always washing his hands'. Two days later Reginald Wilberforce produced an even more innocent explanation, claiming that the origin of the epithet was simply the strange circumstance that at Cuddesdon College there had been inscribed on the gate-posts of the main entrance the four letters 'S.O.A.P.'. These, he explained, were the initials of Samuel Oxon (the founder) and Alfred Potts (the first principal). The sobriquet had therefore nothing whatever to do with personal characteristics.

Then came 'A.H.', writing from the Athenæum, who recalled an episode in the Carlton Club 'some forty years past', when Lord Strangford, renowned for his ready wit, admitted his embarrassment at being overheard using the phrase 'soapy Sam' by the Bishop's brother (Robert again). He thereupon ventured the spontaneous explanation that all he had meant by it was 'that the Bishop, though often in hot water, always came out of it with clean hands'.

James Bateman, on 6 January, endeavoured to rule out the 'four-letter theory'. He recalled seeing the term in print in 1847, applied by 'some of the Bishop's High Church friends to his behaviour in the Hampden affair'.

> A year or two later, while the National Club was still located in the Old Palace yard, I well remember the late Mr Frewen calling out to a brother M.P., 'Won't you come and hear Soapy Sam?', who was to preach that morning… Now, whatever the precise date of the Bishop's sermon, it must at all events have been anterior (i) to the removal of the National Club to its present site in Whitehall

Gardens and (ii) to the building of Cuddesdon College, which did not begin before the year 1853.

Finally, 'J.F.G.', writing on the same day, pushed the origin of the sobriquet even further back.

> I was a boy at Rugby in 1845, in my 16th year, and used occasionally to go over, on whole holidays, to Elmden, the rectory of Mrs Tait's father. Being there soon after Dean Wilberforce's appointment to the See of Oxford, before his consecration, I remember hearing his promotion talked of, how I ventured to ask 'Is that the man they call Soapy Sam?' and how my youthful presumption received a grave but very kindly rebuke from Archdeacon Spooner. Not a stone of Cuddesdon College had been laid at this time.

Now what do all these individual reminiscences tell us? Their accuracy is admittedly somewhat doubtful. It seems *prima facie* unlikely that Robert Wilberforce should have inadvertently overheard two different persons in two different circumstances gossiping about his brother and that he should have reacted in two entirely different ways. Almost certainly two separate anecdotes have sprung from a single episode. It is also probable that A.H. (Augustus Hare?) was claiming for Lord Strangford a readier wit – in this particular instance – than that nobleman could command. All other versions of the story ascribe the witticism about hot water and clean hands to the Bishop himself. The story is told in much more detail in the *Pall Mall Gazette* of 28 October 1865, where the Bishop is alleged to have offered this explanation to a chance female companion while travelling by train to attend a Church Congress at Norwich.

One point, however, emerges clearly. Four out of five correspondents testify to the currency of the term in the 1840s. The 'four-letter theory', ingenious though it is, is therefore quite fanciful and the 'S.O.A.P.' on the gates at Cuddesdon must have been the work of an inspired practical joker or a well-intentioned ass. We may also rule out the explanation given by Francis Legge, in the *Dictionary of National Biography*, that the nickname was 'finally fastened upon [the Bishop] in consequence of Lord Westbury's description in the House of Lords (15 July 1864) of his Synodical judgment on *Essays and Reviews* as 'a well-lubricated set of words, a sentence so oily and saponaceous that no one can grasp it'. There can be little doubt that Westbury chose his words so that the champion of orthodoxy should be immediately recognised.

Further evidence of the early origin of the term is supplied by Trollope. In *The Warden*, published in December 1854, the three sons of Archdeacon Grantly – Charles James (of stiff decorum), Henry (brilliant and pugnacious) and Samuel ('dear little Soapy') – are plainly caricatures of Bishops Blomfield of London, Phillpotts of Exeter and Wilberforce of Oxford. We are also beholden to Trollope for giving us a description of the characteristics, which the sobriquet was intended to convey.

> Samuel was the general favourite ... As engaging a child as ever fond mother petted. He was soft and gentle in his manner, and attractive in his speech; the tone of his voice was melody, every action was a grace; unlike his brothers, he was courteous to all, he was affable to the lowly, and meek even to the scullery maid ... His brothers, however, were not particularly fond of him; they would complain to their mother that Soapy's civility all meant something; they thought that his voice was too often listened to … To speak the truth, Samuel was a cunning boy, and those even who loved him best could not but own that for one so young, he was too adroit in choosing his words, and too skilled in modulating his voice.

This describes very faithfully the popular image of Samuel Wilberforce in the late 1840s. He was the youngest of the bishops on the bench; until 1848 he was much favoured at Court. He had inherited from his father the beautiful speaking-voice, the exquisite manners and charm which had served to make his most forthright opponents seem by comparison gruff and ill-bred. His eloquence was the chief quality that attracted the ecclesiastical talent-spotters. Ten weeks of incessant speaking and preaching during a mission organised by the Society for the Propagation of the Gospel in 1839 was the first demonstration of this power. As a result he was invited to speak on the work of the Society at the Mansion House in April 1840 in the presence of the Lord Mayor, the Archbishop and several other dignitaries. Success on that occasion led him to Exeter Hall to speak in the presence of Prince Albert. Six months later he was invited to court.

Then there was his tact. At a time of fierce conflict within the Church, Samuel – it was widely felt – was a little too eager to eschew party ties. He was moderately Evangelical (so it seemed) and favoured as such by Bishop Sumner; he was moderately Tractarian, but he would have no truck with Froude's *Remains* or *Tract XC*, and would not support his former friend, Isaac Williams, devoted disciple of Keble, in the contest for the Poetry Professorship at Oxford in 1842. These attitudes do not necessarily brand Wilberforce as either inconsistent or insincere. The passionate loyalties which the times evoked and the fact that Samuel, almost alone among his friends, was chosen for substantial preferment gave grounds, however, for the supposition that he was always cautious and occasionally adroit.

During the 1840s – even before he became a bishop – he was mocked in the Press as 'slippery Sam',[5] apparently the original form of the popular epithet. Even some of his later admirers felt uneasy about him. William Palmer confessed

> that for many years I did not feel any confidence in Wilberforce. He seemed to me to court popularity too much – to be willing to become 'all things to all men' too far; to make the world too much the object of his admiration.

The event, however, which established the sobriquet for all time, was the Hampden affair of 1847-8. R. D. Hampden, Regius Professor of Divinity at Oxford (whose appointment to that chair in 1835 had been the occasion of a furious onslaught by the Tractarians on his alleged heterodox teaching in his Bampton lectures of 1832) was nominated by Lord John Russell to the bishopric of Hereford in the autumn of 1847. A howl of protest went up from High Churchmen throughout the country against what was deemed to be a calculated insult on the part of the Prime Minister and a horrifying demonstration of the want of catholicity within the Anglican Church. Since the centre of the opposition to Hampden was, naturally enough, the diocese of Oxford, Samuel Wilberforce seized the opportunity to prove himself a peacemaker, while at the same time trying desperately to fulfil the aspirations of those dearest to him in his own circle (Robert and Henry, his brothers, and also Manning) whose allegiance to the Church of England had been shaken by Newman's secession. He first of all sanctioned Letters of Request initiating proceedings against Hampden in the Court of Arches for teaching false doctrine, subsequently withdrawing his permission on discovering that he had exceeded his authority. He made several efforts to secure a recantation, all of which failed. He then incurred great censure by publicly declaring that he had applied himself 'to a thorough and impartial examination of the Bampton Lectures' and had come to the conclusion 'that they did not justly warrant those suspicions of unsoundness to which they have given rise, and which, so long as I trusted to selected extracts, I myself shared'.[6]

A recitation of the bare facts does scant justice both to Samuel Wilberforce's handling of the case and to his good intentions. Certainly little justice was done at the time. There was much unseemly crowing over 'soapy Sam's' debacle. Charles Greville (who found a new epithet for the Bishop) expressed the general feeling with characteristic bluntness:

> Above all things, Sly Sam of Oxford … has covered himself with ridicule and disgrace. The disgrace is the greater because everybody sees through his motives; he has got into a scrape at Court and is trying to scramble out of it; there, however, he is found out, and his favour seems to have been long waning.[7]

There is no doubt that Samuel Wilberforce was ambitious; perhaps the more so because of his brothers, Robert and Henry, who were so clearly devoid of any interest in self-advancement.[8] This last fact is important because it explains in part the frequency with which Samuel – in letters to his brothers – encouraged them to take advantage of opportunities of preferment, which a casual reader might suppose to be an indication of Samuel's own preoccupation with worldly cares. Thus he wrote to Robert in October 1837 about seeking support to procure the wealthy living of Tunbridge Wells for Henry: 'As to taking a step – I would not *force* or even *humour* the leadings of God's Providence, but it is a part of them to use natural openings.'[9] He was particularly anxious to combat the influence of Newman and Keble on his two brothers, most especially the notion (derived largely from Newman) that 'a world where people rise according to *real* merit may be a very good world but it is not *this* in which Providence has put us'.[10] Therefore only the mediocre rise to the top and those of real ability languish in obscurity.

Furthermore, Samuel was conscious of the necessity of 'using natural openings' just because he felt that he and his two clerical brothers lacked certain advantages which others might possess. When Robert wrote to him in 1840, congratulating him on his appointment to the Archdeaconry and suggesting the possibility of Peel summoning him to the episcopal bench, Samuel replied:

> All such thoughts I utterly dismiss. If we had the natural political allies which our Father's sons might naturally have had, if poor

> William [the eldest brother] had been other than he is, it would not be an unnatural termination for any us. But—[11]

It would appear that Samuel took certain steps to remedy this deficiency. In 1838 he suggested to Robert that it would be prudent to send a complimentary copy of the biography of their father to the Duke of Wellington since 'I sometimes meet him on public occasions and it might be an advantage to me to have had even that claim to acquaintance'.[12] He was particularly anxious to gain election to the Athenæum, but nervous of the opposition of John Wilson Croker, whom he suspected of being hostile to him ever since the *Quarterly* (to which Croker was one of the chief contributors) had published a damaging review of *The Life of William Wilberforce*. In 1838 Samuel described Croker to Robert as

> a man who has raised himself by doing the dirty work of others – he is clever; but he owes far more to being a clever dung feeder than a clever man; few men would carry talents to *his* Master and therefore he found little competition.[13]

After he had secured his election to the Athenæum by dint of 'silencing Croker',[14] he became Vicar of the important living of Alverstoke, and found Croker – a privy councillor and intimate friend of Sir Robert Peel – amongst his parishioners.[15] His tone thereupon changed. In November 1841 he sent a second description of Croker to his brother, describing him as

> … very kind and amusing. The most singular thing is that in all his remarks on men &c he is very kind. I really think that I have never heard him make an unkind remark on anyone. He is very attentive at Church ….[16]

During 1842 and 1843, Croker and Samuel frequently corresponded, and Samuel's letters, printed in Croker's

Correspondence and Diaries show him anxious to portray himself as a moderate churchman, dissociating himself from the 'essentially un-Church' views of the Evangelicals and the 'essentially non-Anglican' doctrine of the Tractarians,[17] and also a political adherent of Sir Robert Peel.

> I trust that Sir Robert will not yield an inch to this dissenting clamour as to his Education Bill [he wrote to Croker in 1843]. It seems to me the very crisis of the moral power of his government, and deeply anxious as I am for its stability and renown *hereafter*, I watch every step with the keenest anxiety.[18]

It would be rash to surmise from this correspondence that Samuel was deliberately smoothing a path which would lead him to a bishopric. In politics he had always been a Tory; his description of his churchmanship summarized accurately the position which he was consistently to hold. Nor is the changed opinion of Croker necessarily a prudent tergiversation. Samuel was always hasty in judgment and often obliged to reverse his earlier opinions. Although Peel was indeed to make Samuel a bishop, the letter that he wrote to Croker, announcing his decision on the Oxford see, would suggest that he had no prior consultations about Samuel's qualifications. Croker's reply is interesting in that it reflects something of the popular estimate of Samuel at that time:

> You could not have made a better choice – the only personal defect that I can detect in Wilberforce will help him in the business both of his Diocese and the Church at large, namely that he inclines to be over-active and rather too adroit. He is, and deservedly, the most popular person that I have ever known – his zeal is great, but his prudence rides it in a tight bit.[19]

As a young man, Samuel clearly enjoyed his popularity and longed to taste the fruits of high office. Personal tragedies, however, had their chastening effect. In the first place, the death of his young wife Emily in March 1841, at the moment when his ambitions seemed to be nearing fulfilment, wrought a deep and abiding change in his character. The loss of his eldest son, Herbert, in 1856, and the secession to the Roman Church of his three brothers, his brother-in-law (Manning) and his eldest daughter during the 1850s and 1860s were torments which might have paralysed a lesser man. He dedicated his life solely to the cause of the Church. The letters written to Robert during 1845, seemingly his *annus mirabilis*, speak of sorrow not of joy. In August 1845, recently installed as Dean of Westminster, he wrote, 'Here I am as the Dean with my Herbert with me – and here I am having already lived out all that was the dream and hope of my life as far as its joy and pleasure went ...'.[20] Shortly after moving to Cuddesdon Palace, he wrote:

> I rode past all our old scenes ... It had a sort of stifling sense of *past present* which I cannot describe. But all these scenes which go back beyond my great life dream of 1821 [when he fell in love with Emily Sargent] never oppress me with that utter depression of spirit which so many things do now which speak of hopes long cherished and more than fulfilled and again withered and dried and clinging dead over what once they clustered round with such a living energy.[21]

Outwardly he remained the same. The readiness with which he took up arms to defend the Church against Darwin, the authors of *Essays and Reviews* and Bishop Colenso show, however, that it was no longer appropriate to speak of him as 'evasive'. A desire to play to the gallery and a deplorable lapse in manners were the cause of his undoing in the encounter with the evolutionist Huxley at the meeting of the British Association at Oxford in 1860. Completely mistaking the occasion, he taunted Huxley with descent from the apes and received the celebrated *riposte* that such a parentage might be preferable to a descent from a man 'endowed with great ability and splendid position, who should use these gifts to discredit humble seekers after truth'. Samuel's adroitness and tact had deserted him. Thus when Gladstone sent him to Winchester in 1869 he had cause to admonish him privately as follows:

> I am of the opinion … that you must have at one or more times have made observations on persons, perhaps playfully, which have been taken as if they indicated a habit of too free comments or remarks. You will know whether this suggestion can be turned to any account.[22]

Many still called him 'soapy Sam', and applauded his speeches and marvelled at his social charm. They did not see beneath the surface. 'How little do men see us', wrote Samuel to Robert, after his triumphant maiden speech in the House of Lords, 'see the torn heart under the seeming hilarity. May God bring us safely through.'[23]

When Gladstone was told the news of Samuel's death, he shed tears of genuine grief. Then followed a long pause as he strove to find the words to express the contribution. 'He was a great Diocesan', he said, and grieved no more.

VIII

THE ASSAULT ON MAMMON: CHARLES GORE & JOHN NEVILLE FIGGIS

A lecture on the Bishop Gore Memorial Foundation, delivered at Westminster Abbey, 10 November 1965. It was subsequently published in *The Journal of Ecclesiastical History,* Vol XVII, no. 2, October 1966 by Cambridge University Press. I have modified the original text slightly.

VIII

THE ASSAULT ON MAMMON: CHARLES GORE & JOHN NEVILLE FIGGIS

> War! That is the enduring condition of the Church on this earth. That is what the word means when we call her militant. And war means an enemy, an opposing spirit. You can have no warfare without there be two mutually opposing spirits.[1]

This makes an impressive opening to a sermon. It would have served as a summons to a Crusade. And in a sense, so it was—at least in the mind of the preacher, John Neville Figgis, priest of the Community of the Resurrection, when he chose to startle the congregation of All Saints, Margaret Street, by portraying for them the likeness of Antichrist. He was speaking at a time when the rumour of war was clear enough to any mildly sensitive ear; a period of taut nerves and mounting hysteria which coincided, as George Dangerfield maintained in a very forceful book, with the 'strange death of Liberal England', that welter of violent passion and irrational panic which heralded the outbreak of the First World War.[2] But Figgis was not thinking of the excesses of the Suffragettes, or the threat of civil war in Ireland, or the Kaiser, or the movement towards syndicalism. He was speaking as a priest denouncing the whole spirit of his age; as a prophet who sees a vision of doom. To the same congregation, a week later, he did, however, allude to the political crisis in words no less gloomy:

> The splendid spires of the edifice of the western world are crumbling. Catastrophe is threatening. We can almost hear the thunders of the avalanche of war—war on a scale unknown. Hardly does the world even look stable any longer. It is not like the forties of Victorian complacency, but looks all tottering—tottering.[3]

So intense was Figgis' contempt for the values of his generation, that it seems as if he almost welcomed disaster as a mark of divine retribution.

The theme of *De contemptu mundi* – the title of a best-seller in the late middle ages[4] – is a little unfashionable today. We talk now of coming to terms with secularism, of 'involvement' as the supreme Christian duty. We are not too happy about phrases such as 'fighting the Devil and all his works'. This is not necessarily a sign of capitulation. Rather is it a more subtle, and possibly more effective, method of undermining the enemy's position from within. Christ and Antichrist are, after all, perpetually at war, and the shape which the conflict assumes changes with the peculiar circumstances of each age; and the ecclesiastical historian cannot but admire the tactical contortions of which the Church has proved herself capable throughout the ages in withstanding the corruptions of the world. It has been – and is, God willing – her destiny to survive through the most unpropitious of times, and she has devised many ingenious weapons in her armoury. Sometimes she will launch a full frontal assault, brandishing the Cross; at other times, she will employ with consummate skill the doctrine of economy or accommodation, making apparent concessions while not really conceding anything at all: the policy of preserving the kernel while discarding the husk. Over the centuries the Church has certainly learnt the necessity of biding her time.

The nineteenth century threw down a challenge which demanded a totally different response. Anyone who bided his time in the early railway age was in danger of being left far behind, surveying a vanishing trail of smoke. There was movement everywhere, and the Church had somehow to direct it, for one false move, a single failure to grasp an opportunity might allow the initiative to pass to the enemy (the utilitarians, chiefly); and, with an unexpected dynamism, born of genuine and well-founded apprehensions, many churchmen – taking the lead from Oxford and Newman's warning that the trumpet must not sound an uncertain note – responded to the challenge. The ethos of the early Victorian age has been described by Professor W. L. Burn as a 'combination of ... despair with passionate hopes and febrile enthusiasms'. In the words of James Anthony Froude: 'It was an era of new ideas, of swift if silent revolution ... The Church had broken away from her old anchorage ... All were agreed to have done with compromise and conventionalities.'

To Froude, of course, the sense of movement was so inspiriting that he came before long to break away from that anchorage:

> All around us, the intellectual lightships had broken from their moorings and it was then a new and trying experience. The present generation which had grown up in an open spiritual ocean, which has got used to it and has learned to swim for itself, will never know what it is to find the lights all drifting, the compasses all awry, and nothing left to steer by except the stars.[5]

From this passage we might gather that the Church was losing the battle. The adventurous became over-adventurous; the satisfied tended to become self-satisfied. Mid-Victorian complacency, as opposed to the restlessness of the earlier period, is not entirely a figment of the historian's imagination, even though it was never so marked as facile generalisation might give us to suppose. It is significant that the critics of the smugness of these middle years, the first to proclaim open war against materialism and *gemutlichkeit* were, on the whole, those who had only the most tenuous allegiance to the Church. Thomas Carlyle began to splutter against the 'Gospel of Mammonism' in 1843—that 'melancholy creed' with its fear of the Hell of 'Not Succeeding'.[6] Matthew Arnold followed with his exposure of the hollowness of London life: 'its internal canker of *publice egestas privatim opulanter* unequalled by the world'.[7]

After 1850 a series of unhappy truths had to be faced: the incapacity of the Church to reach the urban masses; the drift from Christianity of the most able intellects who might have become great leaders of the Church. Even the call to mission gradually became somehow secularised, the attraction of empire-building proving more seductive than saving souls. By the 1880s and 1890s, the Victorian age was effectively over. Society, conventions, fashions, ideals had all become Edwardian before the Prince of Wales had entered upon his heritage. The sobriety of the earlier age had given way to opulence; moral earnestness had degenerated, on the one hand, into a superior type of humanism, which was already beginning to brand religious zeal as hypocritical and – on the other – into a ruthless exploitation for materialistic ends. The old taboos were cast aside; new idols took their place. The Church was again thrown on to the defensive.

The same thing was happening on the continent, notably in France. After 1870, the Catholic Church all over Europe was fighting a battle to preserve its rights against the policy of spoliation and secular control, which was common to the governments of that period. But far worse than this was the pervading spirit of the time, the extravagance and decadence of *la belle époque*, which added a new phrase to the European vocabulary – significantly, a French one – the expression *fin de siècle*. In his brilliant essay on 'The Decay of Idealism in France', delivered originally in lecture form in 1911, J. E. C. Bodley noted with alarm the gradual stifling of national genius under the weight of materialism and mechanisation. The French were forgetting how to talk:

> To hasten the decay of conversation the French have adopted the resources of duller nations for killing time. In Parisian houses and in rural chateaux, the bridge-tables set up in salons, which have been the scene of many a brilliant colloquy, are sad signs of the descent of the wittiest society in the world to the level of the stolid Anglo-Saxon. Even in England the unsociable tyranny of the

modern card-table is to be regretted – but infinitely less than in France. [8]

Society was dominated by cold-hearted financiers; the great cities of Europe were being transformed into 'gaudy pleasure resorts'.[9] Their inhabitants gave one no confidence in the future of western society. 'The men, the women, their dresses, their laughter all spoke of a world not of ideas but of material modern luxury.'[10] We call to mind de Gaulle's description of France in the 1890s, recovering from the hysteria of the Panama scandal – 'like the Infanta weeping in the Palace Gardens, overcome with melancholy, while enjoying the good things of life'.[11]

What had the Church to say? On all accounts she seemed to be the loser. When the young cried out for emancipation, they usually meant freedom from the code of values which the Church had imposed. The rich could have little to do with her, because they despised her moralisms and distrusted her knowledge of economics. The intellectuals were afraid of losing face by coming to her for comfort. In England, at least, they preferred to propound the potentialities of the modern 'higher man'. In the words of Oliver Lodge, written in 1904:

> The higher man of today is not worrying about his sins at all. As for Original Sin or Birth Sin, or other notions of that kind, that sits lightly on him. As a matter of fact, it is non-existent, and no one but a monk could have invented it.[12]

Thus did Antichrist seem to tighten his hold on Edwardian England, showing himself without shame in many guises. His favourite manifestation however, was in the shape of Mammon. The Victorians had sometimes bowed their heads before his shrine, but had done so secretly, knowing they were doing wrong. By the turn of the century all sense of conscience seemed to have dulled. The plutocrat revelled in his irresponsibility. Greed had become his creed, and he was not afraid to say so. 'There are two things necessary to salvation', proclaimed Andrew Undershaft in Shaw's *Major Barbara,* written in 1907: 'Money and Gunpowder'. Professor Cusins expressed a mild surprise: 'That is the general opinion of our governing classes. The novelty is in hearing any man confess it.'[13] Shaw portrayed it on the stage; Miss Sackville-West mocked it in her languorous prose: the pampered waxworks, tired and bored, sated and effete. They had left life long behind and found satisfaction in artifice alone. In such a way did real people become puppets, the playthings of an evil God.[14]

C. F .G. Masterman probed down to the roots of this *malaise*, and was bold enough to put the blame on high society. In gluttony, extravagance and reckless speculation, the Court circle set the worst example of all. And what could one expect from those whom the King chose to be his friends? 'Financial magnates of mediocre minds', as Canon Roger Lloyd described them,[15] playboys and ex-Gaiety Girls, with a common passion for the Turf. Christians and thinking people, who were not dazzled by the tawdry brilliance of this tasteless exhibitionism, or subdued by its brazen arrogance, were revolted. It is to their credit that they frequently protested. From the pen of G. K. Chesterton came the picture of 'The Maniac', the materialist of insane simplicity, over whose cell in the asylum to which he consigns himself shall be written, with dreadful truth 'He believes in himself.'[16] It is the rejection of this aristocratic boorishness and heartless irresponsibility, which lies behind the persistent efforts of the Christian Social Union to obtain some measure of social justice. In founding the Community of the Resurrection, Charles Gore made his own enduring protest against the unbridled materialism of the *fin de siècle* and the values of Edwardian society. But none was so forthright as John Neville Figgis. In him the sense of urgency, which throbs right through the nineteenth century, reaches its strident climax. The world must know the direction in which it is moving. Never was there greater need to decide between the way of the world and the way of the Cross.

Historians seem to have concurred with these denunciations. We must always remember how perilous it is to judge an age from the standpoint of the Jeremiads which it invoked; and many an historian, in playing the role of an Actonian judge, has succeeded merely in presenting an unconscious image of himself. What we castigate in the past is, too often, only a revelation of what disturbs us in the present. Nevertheless, there is much truth in the strictures of Roger Lloyd when he writes:

> The gospel of God's indiscriminating and fathomless love holds no syllable of comfort for the complacent and the proud. There has seldom existed a generation of English people which more needed and less desired the Christian Redemption.[17]

Chesterton—Gore—Figgis. They make a strange trio and yet they were all trying to say the same thing, albeit in differing ways. Chesterton, that master of sustained paradox, whose devastating wit is as unfashionable today – alas – as the plays of Bernard Shaw or the novels of Arnold Bennett, was always ready to have a tilt at Mammon. What horrified him above all else was the enormous effrontery of man. Gore, too, took this as his theme in the last sermon that he preached in the nineteenth century, heralding the year 1901 in terms of deep despondency. The subject was 'the hollowness of modern progress' and the strange delusions of man's grandeur which came from baseless pride and self-satisfaction.[18] Figgis frequently made the same point, comparing modern society to the rough and cruel world of the Middle Ages, which yet exhibited far more evidence of rightness of heart than the bleakly avaricious conceits of his own generation. The Holy Roman Empire broke down, he admitted, 'under the passion and the pride of man'. But at least it was an honest attempt to achieve something noble and to the glory of God. Not so today. He wrote:

The statecraft, the economics, the education, the literature, the social and family life of our day are organised on a basis frankly secular. So far as these things are concerned, we might almost say that God does not count. Consequently it is the symbols of material possession that are alone striking in the world of today.[19]

Gore and Figgis had more in common than this protest against the hollowness of modern progress. There were similarities both in the particular criticisms and their understanding of the proper cure. Both saw the way of salvation in terms of personal sacrifice and renunciation; the recovery of something which the modern Church had perhaps lost sight of – the spirit of selfless dedication to a cause, the sense of fellowship or brotherhood, the power of service, discipline and love. It was to seek all these things and to encourage them in others that Gore founded the Community of the Resurrection in July 1892; and it was to share these benefits and to discover for himself the salutary effects of deliberate renunciation that Figgis joined the community at Mirfield in 1907, having been converted to the monastic ideal – surely an unique occurrence – while watching a play by Bernard Shaw.[20]

Then again, both men felt an intense repugnance to the heartlessness and callousness of contemporary society. This was not only a hatred of the cruelties inflicted in the name of competition and commercial interest – the fearful revelations of the treatment of the Chinese coolies in the goldmines of the Transvaal, or the ghastly picture drawn by Roger Casement of labour conditions on the rubber plantations[21] – but rather a profound distrust of the motives or the Establishment as a whole. Gore had an exalted conception of the office of bishop; but he was far from being an Establishment man. There was a part of him which responded with sympathy to Frere's famous jibe: 'really Westminster Abbey is enough to stifle any one's religion'.[22] The real problem was that the basis of the Establishment was property.

Thus he contrasted the laws laid down by Christ in the Sermon on the Mount with the legal system of the contemporary world. The true principle of justice, he wrote, is 'that each individual man is an end, and not a mere means: or, that each man counts one, and nobody more than one'. It is a principle 'not approximately realized in what we call Christian society at present'.[23] Law is more concerned with the protection of property than the protection of people.[24] We have reverted – he would seem to be saying – to the definition of the sophist Thrasymachus in Book One of Plato's *Republic* – 'just' and 'right' mean nothing but what is 'in the interest of the stronger party'.

That Figgis felt the same is well known. He devoted a whole chapter to the vice of 'Legalism' in his *Some Defects in English Religion,* published in 1917;[25] and, in his most famous and greatest book – *Churches in the Modern State* – published in 1913, he introduced his subject by a vehement attack on the terrible injustice implicit in two recent legal judgments (Taff Vale and the Free Church of Scotland Appeals case). 'More and more is it clear,' he wrote, 'that the mere individual's freedom against an omnipotent State may be no better than slavery.' And at the root of it all was Mammon again:

> More and more must we have on our side all who are not dazzled by the cry of efficiency or sunk into that un-Christian materialism which has been the consequence in the more comfortable classes of the long security of England and her vast wealth.[26]

A clergyman pontificating from the pulpit on public events is not always an edifying sight; and a concourse of them discussing papers on wages and profits was not likely to extract from the Andrew Undershafts of the Edwardian world, or the genuine radicals among the working classes, more than a passing glance of contempt. The Christian Social Union, founded by Henry Scott Holland with the active support of Westcott and Gore, was doubtless 'mild and watery' to a man like Conrad

Noel;[27] it talked too much and acted too little; much of what it talked about seemed naïve to the expert or intrusive ineptitude to the business man. But from its inception it was meant to stand as a witness, to serve as 'a tardy act of repentance' (as Gore himself put it) for past lethargy, for permitting 'the economic and industrial world to build itself up on quite fundamentally unchristian premisses'.[28] To Gore and Figgis this concern for politics was not an occasional descent from Olympus; it was an essential part of their Christian thought, inseparable, we may say, from Gore's incarnational thelogy and Figgis' understanding of the relationship between Church and State. They castigated the world, but were never aloof from it. It is typical of Figgis, for instance, that he should preface his William Belden Noble lectures at Harvard with the observation: 'I write this on the day of the introduction of the Bill for a Minimum Wage.'[29]

Both were socialists – of a sort. As far back as the famous Bampton Lectures of 1891 (on the Incarnation), Gore wrote:

> The remedies proposed for the evils of society have generally a more or less 'socialistic' character. Now by socialism is commonly meant a certain political theory as to the function of the state in controlling the freedom of individual citizens in the acquisition and employment of wealth ... I may, however, confess myself to be among those who would somewhat jealously set limits to the paternal supervision of the democratic state. But there is another sort of socialism, wholly voluntary, or dependent only upon spiritual sanctions, which the doctrine of the Incarnation seems, beyond all question, to bring with it. There exists what can rightly be called a Christian socialism, by the very fact that the law of brotherhood is the law of Christ.[30]

This was a socialism which had nothing to do with Marx, which rejected all materialistic interpretation of the political doctrine, and which sought always to emphasise social and political duties rather than rights.[31] If we look for its roots, we shall find ourselves in the Oxford of T. H. Green. All the *Lux Mundi* group, all those who began their joint discussions on theology and morals in the sessions of the Holy Party at Oxford in the early 1870s had been profoundly influenced by Green's *Lay Sermons* with their stern rejection of hedonism and their passionate call to altruism. They all came to see democracy and socialism as historical movements working to the end of the universal brotherhood of man. They could not resist Green's appeal for assistance. Steeped as they were in the poetry of Robert Browning – for this generation worshipped Browning as their fathers had venerated Wordsworth – they felt the need of some great cause, some magnificent challenge demanding dedication and self-sacrifice. We find something of the same spirit – altruism combined with the thrill of unfettered intellectual enquiry – in the Cambridge of Henry Sidgwick. Some followed their master into a peculiar brand of earnest agnosticism; others found the challenge they were seeking in the London slums. For Gore and his friends the answer lay in a complete re-orientation of the Gospel message. Self-fulfilment could not be divorced from social obligation; and as Melvin Richter has put it, 'personality, to be fully realised, must not be subjected to the so-called iron law of economics, but to the moral requirements of the Church'.[32]

Figgis' socialism was akin to guild-socialism. On one occasion, indeed he confessed to Sir Ernest Barker that he was a syndicalist.[33] Time and again in his writings, he makes the assertion that the modern state system is based on a complete misconception. In contemporary society the state is represented as the Great Leviathan, jealous of all other Gods, denying the right of corporate independence to the lesser groups within it. 'Now the State did not create the family, nor did it create the Churches; nor even in any real sense can it be said to have created the Club or the trades unions.' These have all, he goes on to say, 'arisen out of the natural associative instincts of mankind'.[34] Not surprisingly, Figgis was a staunch supporter of the 'Life and Liberty' movement, which represented far more accurately than the Christian Social Union his own particular aims.

Gore and Figgis protested against the evils of twentieth-century society for rather different reasons. A closer examination reveals other differences, too. In temperament they were poles apart; and they had been formed by very different influences. Everything we know of Gore suggests that he was, as Newman had been, a rare example of *anima naturaliter Christiana*. By the time he came up to Balliol in 1871, his 'mind was fundamentally and ... quite incurably religious', G. L. Prestige writes.[35] Figgis, by contrast, was a man of volatile spirit, who had sprung from dissenting stock, a lover of good living in his early days and one who had experienced a definite conversion. There is little doubt that he was a manic-depressive, twice suffering from debilitating mental illness. While Gore was a theologian, Figgis was an historian—and a peculiarly favoured one, having been trained at different stages of his Cambridge career by Mandell Creighton, Lord Acton and F. W. Maitland. All three left some mark upon him. Creighton, whom he accounted the greatest man of the three (as opposed to Maitland, 'the greatest historian', and Acton 'the most widely erudite'),[36] taught him independence of judgment and imbued him with a lasting sense of the historic elements of Anglicanism. From Acton, Figgis derived his burning moral passion – his tendency to censoriousness perhaps – and a lifelong fascination for continental philosophy. As a young man he had fallen under the spell of the French philosopher Henri Bergson and had become a Pragmatist. Thence he passed to Nietzsche and reeled under the blow. He would go back to his writings again and again, as a child will torture itself by feeding its mind on some horror picture which haunts its dreams. At one moment Nietzsche appears to him as 'the shining expression of the spirit of Antichrist' with his glorification of pride and philosophy of cruelty.[37] At the next, he seems to show a twisted path to truth in his vicious onslaught upon arid intellectualism, and his concept of 'the transvaluation of all values', which Figgis uses in a Christian context to describe the purpose of the Incarnation: 'to make all things new—a new heaven and a new earth'.[38]

The most powerful German influence upon Figgis – derived from Maitland[39] – was Otto Gierke. Maitland's own studies on the nature of corporations and Gierke's appreciation 'that the real world is composed of several communities, large and small, and that a community is something more than the sum of the persons composing it'[40] brought Figgis, as it did William McDougal, into the philosophy of pluralism; a doctrine which repudiates individualism on the one hand, and State socialism on the other, maintaining the right of groups within the state to develop freely their inherent life and purpose.[41] The influence of Maitland, too, is marked in Figgis's own work in the sphere of medieval history, to which – it must be admitted – he brought a romanticism which was wholly absent from the writings of his mentor. This was a potent factor in Figgis's abhorrence of materialism. His lectures on Armageddon and Babylon in *Civilisation at the Cross Roads* show this clearly: 'The world in the Middle Ages was far enough from the practice of holiness, but at least it did not question the ideal. What are men's ideals today?'[42] Again:

> The Middle Ages had their 'forestallers and regraters' but they did not call them 'kings of finance'... If men did not copy, at least they canonized S. Frances. Nowadays the police would lock him up for sleeping in the open.[43]

Such sentiment is absent from Gore's writings. He was much more temperate in tone. As a child of the Oxford Movement, he had learnt the lesson of 'reserve'. We should not forget that, at heart, Gore was a Tractarian. For all his seeming disloyalty to Liddon through his contribution to *Lux Mundi,* he bore the marks of his kinship with Keble, Newman and Pusey, both in his person and in his writings in a way in which Figgis, for all his high sacramentalism, did not. After all, the adulation of all things medieval was essentially a Cambridge manifestation. It formed no part of the Tractarian tradition which, with its harking back to the Fathers and the Caroline divines, was steeped in patristic learning.

It is, I believe, significant that Figgis tended to look back to the age of St Bernard, while Gore found his inspiration in the Christianity of St Basil. Wherever possible, Gore was wont to appeal to the genius of the Greek Fathers rather than to the tradition of the Latin Church. It seemed to him that the problems of his own day were akin to those which faced the early Christians.

> Certainly [he wrote in his Bampton Lectures] among Christians of the first four centuries ... there was a requirement made on the intelligence and patience of the individual, at least as great as that made by the English Church even in its present condition. And it needs to be remembered, that in appealing across the ages to the Church of the first centuries, we are not appealing merely to a Church which is primitive, but to one which existed under intellectual conditions comparatively like our own.[44]

We could learn from their response to the problem of moral decadence:

> We should do again what was done in the early monastic movement, as it is represented in St Basil's rule. We should draw together to centres, both in town and country, where men can frankly start afresh and live openly the common life of the first Christians ... I have some experience such as warrants a belief that such an ideal may become real.[45]

There is much of Newman in this, indeed an echo of Newman's famous sermon on 'Feasting in Captivity' (September 1842), when he described in stark contrast the differences between the nineteenth century's understanding of the Christian life and that of the early ages of the Church: 'What points in common are there between the easy religion of this day and the religion of St Athanasius and St Chrysostom?'[46]

This teaching brings us to an even earlier influence on Gore, which, because it presented him with just such an ideal at his most impressionable age, made him peculiarly susceptible to what he was to encounter from the Tractarian tradition at Oxford. All writers on the life and work of Gore have observed that while he was a schoolboy at Harrow in the late 1860s he would have known Brooke Foss Westcott, who was then an assistant master on Montagu Butler's staff. He would, for instance, have heard Westcott's moving sermon on 'Disciplined Life', preached in the school chapel in 1868.[47]

The links between Westcott and Gore have not – as far as I know – been explored as fully as they warrant. The most obvious is the similarity of their understanding of the nature of Christian socialism. From early days Westcott had exhibited a touch of radicalism in his social views – ever since he had witnessed as a boy the Chartist riots in the Birmingham Bull Ring. It was part of his nature to abhor extravagance and luxury, and no one – not even T. H. Green himself – could have so powerfully impressed others with the futility of service to Mammon than did Westcott by the pattern of his own life.

The Harrow sermon of 1868 definitely left its mark upon Gore. Westcott chose as his text the passage from the fifth chapter of Ephesians (verse 13): 'Look carefully how ye walk', taking as his theme the power of asceticism and the way in which the Church has throughout all ages defied moral corruption by the ascetic appeal.

> History thus teaches us that social evils must be met by social organisation. A life of absolute and calculated sacrifice is a spring of immeasurable power. In the past it has worked marvels, and there is nothing to prove that its virtue is exhausted.[48]

When Gore was called upon to preach the University Sermon at Oxford on the second Sunday in Advent 1894, he chose exactly the same text: 'Look carefully how ye walk, not as unwise but as wise; buying up the opportunity because the days are evil.' This sermon contains some of Gore's most vehement strictures on Mammon – moral slackness, lawlessness, selfishness, luxury, and the futility of countering these evils by an easy-going religion. It is time to speak 'stern words in the king's sanctuary and the royal house'. Search for the faithful servants of God. 'Where they are, there is the secret of recovery, the hope of revival.'[49]

There is further and perhaps still more striking evidence of a real connection between Westcott and Gore, which again particularly relates to their common hatred of Mammon and the means they proposed to resist its lures. In the late 1860s while Gore was at Harrow, Westcott was becoming more and more attracted by an idea, which had originated in his own mind, of implementing an experiment in reviving the early Christian practice of communal living by establishing a 'Cœnobium'. He outlined his plans to two of his most intimate married friends, Edward White Benson and F. J. A. Hort. Might it not be possible to form 'an association of families, bound together by common principles of living, of work, of devotion, subject during the time of voluntary co-operation to central control, and united by definite obligations?'[50] Both Benson and Hort showed interest in the principle, but felt that it could not work in practice.[51] By the end of 1868 the matter was dropped. It is surely significant, however, that thirty-five years later the proposal re-appears: this time from the pen of Charles Gore. In his pamphlet on the *Social Doctrine of the Sermon on the Mount,* in which Gore invited his contemporaries to return to the ascetic techniques of the age of St Basil, he raised the question of providing opportunities for married people to experience a form of communal living.

> The literal reproduction of the earliest Christian community life ... needs application to married life also. I do not see why such an

ideal as the Moravians have, in fact, realised, of companies of married people living by a common rule, should not be of immense power among ourselves.[52]

The whole point of the experiment would be to demonstrate that Mammon could be dethroned and that real happiness can come from the consciousness that his thraldom has been resisted. Westcott's own avowed aims were 'the conquest of luxury, the disciplining of intellectual labour, the consecration of every fragment of life by religious exercises'.[53]

What else might Westcott have taught Gore? His enduring love for the Greek Fathers, perhaps; his devotion to the philosophy of Plato, well established by the time he had become a fellow of Trinity College, Oxford? It is arguable that his distrust of the Catholic Modernists, with their Aristotelian preoccupation with ends rather than beginnings, sprang from this source. Westcott's teaching pointed in the same direction. The best guide to his own religious philosophy is his *History of Religious Thought in the West,* published in 1891, which traces the development of Platonic ideas through the medium of Christian theology.[54] This is not to discount the influence of T. H. Green on Gore. It does, however, appear that when he left Harrow for Oxford, Gore was already well-prepared to imbibe Green's views. Neither the tendencies of thought nor the attitude to moral problems which he encountered at Oxford were new to him. They were rather a striking confirmation of teaching he had received at school.

But we must take a last look at Mammon. The Edwardian monster was slain in due course; though not, one would have to admit, by the darts which Gore and Figgis, and others like them, had aimed at his tough, unyielding hide, He was killed during the social and political upheavals which followed in the wake of the First World War. But before he died, he spawned. Figgis noticed the danger in his Harvard Lectures.[55] Gore discerned the first signs of it in his University Sermon of 1894.[56] Mammonism was beginning to permeate all classes. The creed of Greed, the pursuit of comfort as an end in itself, the battle for status, assessed by the accumulation of material possessions; these are the pockmarks of a spreading infection, erupting now in suburbia, now in the housing estate. The phenomenon acquires a high-sounding name: the Affluent Society, which neither Gore nor Figgis would have hesitated to use as a term of abuse. They, however, are no longer with us. The challenge has to be met by new opponents. The battle with Antichrist goes on, and so it is that the prophets and leaders of the Church of their posterity have to ponder anew their interpretation of the text of the Epistle to the Ephesians: 'Look therefore carefully how ye walk … because the days are evil.'

IX

THE NOVELS OF CHARLES DICKENS: FACT AND FICTION

This paper was a contribution to a conference on 'Victorian Life and Culture', held at the Bishop Otter Centre in Chichester on 13 October 2001.

IX

THE NOVELS OF CHARLES DICKENS: FACT AND FICTION

Chichester, 13 October 2001

Charles Dickens died on 9 June 1870. On the next day, the *Daily News* paid him the following tribute: 'He was emphatically the novelist of his age. In his pictures of contemporary life posterity will read, more clearly than in contemporary records, the character of nineteenth-century life.' A few years later an admirer observed: 'He was the man of his epoch and had the spirit-time throbbing within him.' Historians and literary critics of our own day, however, have tended to cast doubt on the actual value of Dickens' novels as authentic guides to either the life or the culture of his own time. They constitute a 'primary source' for Dickens' life, Humphrey House has suggested; beyond that, the supposedly factual content should be handled, if not with scepticism, at least with a great deal of care.

In one respect, this counsel of caution cannot be challenged. Nothing that Dickens wrote, even in his more polemical productions as a journalist, actually influenced the course of nineteenth-century history. Although he frequently aimed to arouse a sense of outrage at public and social scandals – such as the brutality of the infamous 'Yorkshire schools' (in *Nicholas Nickleby*), or the inhumane workings of the New Poor Law (in *Oliver Twist*), or the appalling inefficiency of the conduct of the Crimean War (in *Little Dorrit*), or the scandalous neglect of sanitary reform and Public Health (in *Bleak House*) – he never actually instigated or initiated any particular reform. The most that could be said of his influence was that, through his novels, he gained more and more public sympathy for the causes that he espoused and his simple philosophy of natural, human benevolence as the panacea for all ills.

Nevertheless it is prudent to be equally sceptical about the lofty omniscience that historians sometimes claim in their reappraisal of contemporary observations of their times. It is certainly true that an historian has one great advantage over the consequences of events that seemed significant, or otherwise, at any particular time. He can unearth evidence that was not then available and can chart, from a different perspective, probable causes and certain effects. But, however conscientious and perceptive a historian may be, there are certain things that must elude him for the want of a guide as acutely observant and incomparably talented in descriptive writing as Dickens: things such as the actual speech of men and women at the time, the smell of early Victorian London, the little idiosyncrasies of dress, mannerisms and expressions—all priceless vignettes which serve to bring the past back to vibrant life.

But is Dickens always reliable? There were undoubtedly areas of the life, character and culture of his time where Dickens, because of his personal circumstances, background and prejudices, had to rely on imagination rather than observation. Often the plots of his novels required him to stray outside the range of his actual experience, and therefore his characterisation becomes weak and unconvincing. He was not at home in, and certainly not in sympathy with, high society. When he became famous he sometimes had to mingle with the aristocracy, but he never felt comfortable in such company, aware that he occasionally betrayed his relatively humble background by solecisms such as combing his hair in public or lapsing into an unguarded Cockneyism. By his own admission he preferred to be 'a king in low company' rather than a misfit among the high and mighty. Hence his depiction of aristocratic rakes like Sir Mulberry Hawk and Lord Frederick Verisopht is suggestive of melodrama, and the tinselly affectations of the social circle of the Veneerings in *Our Mutual Friend* (with the exception of the inspired invention of Mr Podsnap) strain Dickens' attempt at humour to the limit and he becomes arch and facetious.

Then again, one can hardly regard Dickens as a sure guide to the religious history of the nineteenth century, indisputably one of the most significant developing themes of the successive decades of his lifetime. Gladstone, we are told, had no high opinion of *Nicholas Nickleby* 'because there was no Church in it'. But whenever the Church or Churches figure in subsequent novels, the picture is entirely distorted by Dickens' own childhood experiences and by his ingrained prejudices. Early memories of being 'dragged by the hair of my head' to attend services at the Baptist chapel in Chatham and forced 'to be steamed like a potato in the unventilated breath of the powerful Boanerges Boiler and his congregation' endowed Dickens with an enduring horror of Dissenting preachers and puritanical self-righteous Evangelicals. If the oily Mr Chadband, declaiming the 'tru-weth' to poor Jo, the crossing-sweeper, in *Bleak House* is the funniest and most savage of his caricatures, the propensity of silly middle-aged or elderly women to tax their husbands or families with pious moralisms drawn from the Protestant Manual (like Mrs Varden), or from study of the Good Book (like Mrs Clennam) or with injunctions to be 'born again', which caused Mr Weller senior to make uproarious jokes to Young Sam, was one of Dickens' favourite Aunt Sallies.

One of the most unforgivable sins of the Evangelicals, to Dickens' thinking, was their almost Malthusian determination to condemn and restrict the innocent amusement of the lower classes. He violently opposed Sir Andrew Agnew's Sunday Observance Bill of 1836, and – in *Little Dorrit* – put much of his own mind in Arthur Clennam's reflections on the miserable dullness of an English Sunday as he returned home from abroad. By contrast, Dickens in *Hard Times* delights in the sense of uninhibited enjoyment as manifested in Mr Sleary's circus troupe and that good man's lisping declaration that 'People mutht be amuthed'.

The whole Evangelical concept of charity was anathema to Dickens. On the one hand there were the misdirected efforts of missionary societies, showing more concern for absurdly distant beneficiaries than for the crying need of the destitute at home, caricatured in Mrs Jellyby in *Bleak House*; on the other hand there was the cold and patronising charity that invested the recipient with a stigma. Rob the Grinder, despatched by Mr Dombey to the Bluecoat School, nurtures lasting resentment at the consequent jeering of his former associates, and Mrs Pardiggle by her instrusive visits to the lowly brickmaker's family becomes yet another of Dickens' figures of fun. None of this is entirely fictitious, of course. Everybody recognised the infelicitous aspect of this sort of giving, abundantly testified by the proliferation of charitable societies during the early nineteenth century. Dickens' hatred of it, and his suspicion of the hypocrisy and humbug that lay behind much of it, received its fullest expression in the person of Mr Honeythunder in *Edwin Drood* whose religious dogmatism became the more intolerable because of its association with the worst impersonal aspects of utilitarianism.

Of course there is more to the religious history of the nineteenth century than this, but one would hardly suppose so from reading Dickens' novels. No mention of the Oxford Movement, for instance, except a suggestion of Puseyism in Mrs Pardiggle. Dickens actually had no high opinion of the Roman Church, despite his sympathetic treatment of at least one of its adherents, in the person of Mr Haredale in *Barnaby Rudge*. As for the Established Church, there is only a single mention of a well-run parish – that of Mr Milvey in *Our Mutual Friend*. It is not that Dickens was an irreligious man. For a while he attended services at a Unitarian Chapel. He was anxious that his children were brought up as Christians. The essence of his own creed was to follow the Sermon on the Mount. 'I hold our Saviour to be the model of all goodness', he once wrote. His words as recorded in the New Testament were all-sufficient.

Deep down, Dickens' dislike of dogmatic preacher and religious 'know-alls' arose from his aversion to all forms of authority in a position to impose upon himself. By nature authoritative within his own chosen circle, and a great upholder of law and order as administered by the Police, he had no time for self-important dignitaries such as judges and magistrates. His fictional schoolmasters, too, are rarely adornments to their profession. Squeers and Creakle are sadistic brutes, Dr Blimber a rather benign eccentric, and Bradley Headstone, the most complex of Dickens' villains, although competent enough within his small and humble realm, is tormented into madness through his lust for Lizzie Haxham and his hatred for the arrogant indifference to his position by Eugene Wrayburn. Dr Strong, who completes David Copperfield's education at Rochester, is exempt from censure or ridicule as also is the poor kind village schoolmaster who gives succour to Little Nell and her grandfather.

Although so much of Dickens' material in his novels was drawn from his personal experience, it is curious how little his books have anything revealing to say about the contemporary political scene, especially since he must have witnessed many important debates in his early years as a parliamentary reporter. In his polemical journalism he allied himself to certain political and social causes – the Repeal of the Corn Laws, for instance, and his *exposé* of the appalling deaths from cholera at the Juvenile Pauper Asylum at Tooting. His novels, on the other hand, while revealing his contempt for the legislature in their neglect of the sufferings of the poor, offer very little positive by way of specific reform. *Little Dorrit* (originally to be titled 'Nobody's Fault') contains a scathing attack on the administrative bureaucracy in his satirical picture of the Circumlocution Office; and the slow-moving Court of Chancery receives similar treatment in *Bleak House*, together with some horrific revelations of the consequence of neglecting sanitary reform and the lethal state of London's graveyards. These were sincere reflections of Dickens' views. But since he regarded the political set-up, as it existed in his time, as dominated by an effete aristocracy, riddled with jobbery and corruption, his only answer was to put his faith in Benevolence. If only everybody could act like the Cheeryble brothers in *Nicholas Nickleby*, or Mr Garland in *The Old Curiosity Shop*, or Mr Brownlow, Mr Jarndyce, Mr Boffin and others of his galaxy of lifesavers, then what a happy place England would become. An excellent creed, no doubt, but hardly a realistic one, given the selfishness of human nature. When Dickens offered this solution to the problems of industrial strife in *Hard Times*, his nostrum was dismissed by critics as hopelessly 'unreal'.

In all the areas examined so far, one would have to admit that a historian would find in Dickens' novels very little that he did not know already or that could not find less emotionally and more factually expressed in other sources. Indeed, any attempt to extract the factual from the fictional in his novels must take into account Dickens' motives for writing and his consciousness of the audience that he was seeking to address. There can surely be no doubt that Dickens was, first and foremost, an entertainer; more than that, he was an entertainer who was obsessively concerned with making as handsome a living as possible from his writings. To use a phrase borrowed from the media of today, he was almost neurotically determined to maintain the high level of his ratings.

From his earliest days, Dickens had been fascinated by the theatre. It had been his ambition at one stage to become an actor, and in his later years the craving was partly gratified by his public reading, delivered in true Victorian histrionic style. His novels abound in theatrical techniques, employed to make his audience cry or laugh uproariously or to grip their seats in thrilling anticipation (one of the reasons, incidentally, why his novels transfer so readily and successfully to the television screen). Hence his predilection for melodrama and melodramatic villains who identify their villainy almost from first appearance. They may range from the grotesquely evil Daniel Quilp to the money-grabbing machinations of a Ralph Nickleby or a Jonas Chuzzlewit, or the manipulative nastiness of Uriah Heep, or the suave craftiness of the blackmailing Tulkinghorn, or the blatant hypocrisy of Pecksniff, but they all tell the reader two things. This way evil comes; and, secondly and most gratifyingly, they will surely get their true deserts in the end. Peter Ackroyd suggests that Dickens' moral philosophy was most simply expressed by J. A. Froude, writing of the lessons of history: 'In the long run all is well with the good; in the long run it is ill with the wicked.' This is exactly what Dickens' readership wanted and expected, and they were never disappointed, even to the extent of Dickens' wish somehow to contrive a satisfying 'Final Curtain' with all the characters who have not been killed off assembling to take their bow. Dickens also knew the importance of introducing stagey character parts, often employing the device of the catchphrase (the stock-in-trade of music hall comedians and old-fashioned radio shows: Sandy Powell's 'Can you hear me, mother?' or ITMA's Mrs Mop, 'Can I do you now, sir?'). So how often will Captain Cuttle say 'When found, make a note of', or Mr Snagsby 'Not to make too fine a point of it' or Mr Toots 'It's of no consequence'—and many, many more? On every appearance of Mrs Gamp in *Martin Chuzzlewit*, readers will be waiting for the word 'dispoged' and recollections of the wise words of the fictitious 'Mrs Harris'.

Did this make Dickens' characters so theatrical that they are little more than caricatures? It would be very rash to go so far as this. Many of his most memorable characters were based on originals whom Dickens had met prior to writing, having noted joyfully their foibles and little idiosyncrasies and seen the potential for accentuating these into something rather larger than life. Even Quilp had an original in a dwarf whom Dickens met in Bath; Sarah Gamp sprang from observing the nurse of a companion of Mrs Burdett-Coutts; Inspector Bucket was drawn from an Inspector Fields whom Dickens had met when visiting the recently established Detective Department of Scotland Yard. Paul Dombey bore a faint resemblance to Dickens' young nephew, Henry Burnett. W. S. Landor and Leigh Hunt appear in *Bleak House*, as Boythorne and Harold Skimpole. This was far from kind to Leigh Hunt, and Dickens found himself in a spot of trouble when Mrs Hill detected her identity in the little chiropodist, Miss Mowcher, in *David Copperfield*. It is even suggested that the idea of Podsnap came from observing the occasional dogmatic pomposities of his future biographer, John Forster. Of course, Dickens' irresistible sense of the comic led to distortion. But his readers at the time, as well as in his posterity, would not have wished it otherwise. Even though some of these characters were entirely unnecessary to the plots of his novels, Dickens was well aware that they guaranteed their sales.

Two of Dickens' most endearing characters – Wilkins Micawber and Mark Tapley – appear to have no originals, and their respective attitudes to life stretch one's credulity to the limit. Can anyone have been so genially improvident as Micawber or so determined to prove his jolliness in the direst of circumstances as Mark Tapley? John Dickens, the novelist's father, was hopelessly improvident but far from genial, and yet it was from his father's lips, on the occasion of his incarceration in the Marshalsea, that Dickens received the advice that will ever remain as the most celebrated of all Micawberisms: 'Annual income twenty pounds, annual expenditure nineteen pounds nineteen and six, result happiness. Annual income twenty pounds, annual expenditure twenty pounds ought and six, result misery.' Dickens' fiction is never entirely divorced from fact. Tapley has no original that has been traced, but Dickens stole his name from a church register in Chatham many years before he came to write *Chuzzlewit*.

Was it Dickens' sense of the theatrical – he knew his Shakespeare well, and how frequently the character of the 'fool' appeared in his plays – or was it his own fascination with deformity, both physical and mental, that caused him so often to introduce those whom we might describe as 'simples' into his novels? Barnaby Rudge was actually a 'natural'—Mrs Rudge's 'idiot son'; Mr Dick in *Copperfield* lived in his little world of flying kites and trying to trace King Charles' head, but Betsy Trotwood flattered him by always turning to him for advice on David's upbringing. Jennie Wren in *Our Mutual Friend*, with her bad back and queer legs as well as strange fancies, had instant perception of the evil in Bradley Headstone and the warm heart of Eugene Wrayburn; Sloppy, too, another simple who liked to work away at Betty Higden's mangle, was given the privilege of delivering the *coup-de-grâce* to the wooden-legged rogue Silas Wegg by flinging him in a mud cart. Mr Chuffy in *Chuzzlewit*, Little Dorrit's friend, Maggie, and – of course – the badly deformed Smike, all touch the heart in their simplicity. They all in their way exhibit Dickens' philosophy, so attractive to his essentially middle-class readership: goodness is the property of the gentle and ingenuous people, characters like Tom Pinch, Bob Cratchit, Kit Nubbles or Newman Noggs.

It is when Dickens strays from the comic, grotesque or simple and ingenuous characters of his supporting cast in his books that he tends to fall into the far less effective stereotypes of his heroines – pure, angelic, young and beautiful, all evocation of his passionate love for his sister-in-law, Mary Hogarth, who died at the age of 17 (Little Nell, Ruth Pinch, Amy Dorrit, Florence Dombey and Agnes Wickfield). Middle and old age tends to turn women either into frumps like Sally Brass in *The Old Curiosity Shop*, or garrulous naggers like Mrs Wilfer, Mrs Varden or Mrs Macstinger. One frump, at least was cruelly drawn from life. Maria Beadnell, Dickens' first love, had, when Dickens chose to meet her in middle age, become by her own admission 'toothless, fat, old and ugly'; and she appears as exactly that as Flora Finching in *Little Dorrit*.

Again, because Dickens was so conscious of maintaining his readership, especially within the family circle, he became as anxious as Mr Podsnap to avoid bringing 'a blush to the cheek of the young person'. All Dickens' courtships are sedulously coy and chaste. Time and again one or other of the partners, if not both, maintain a sort of fiction that their relationship is really that of brother and sister; so with Florence Dombey and Walter Gay, and Rose Budd and Edwin Drood, and David Copperfield and Agnes Wickfield. This tells Dickens' readers that sooner or later wedding bells will ring, but sometimes that conclusion is aggravatingly slow in coming, as – of instance – when David persists in regarding poor Agnes as 'a stained-glass window'. Very rarely does Dickens allow ugly sexual impulses to be hinted at, such as Quilp's lust for Little Nell, or the gloating anticipation of the odious Hugh in *Barnaby Rudge* when he has both Dolly Varden and Emma Haredale entirely in his power.

There are few exceptions to Dickens' idealised portrait of young womanhood. Neither Bella Rokesmith nor Estella in *Great Expectations* quite fit the stereotype while having in common the admission that they 'have no heart'. The fact that Bella is so determined not to be 'a doll in a doll's house' (where Dickens normally liked his heroines to reside) perhaps suggest that at the time when *Our Mutual Friend* was written, Dickens was becoming aware of a rather changed attitude towards the expected domesticity of the female state. As for Estella, Dickens had originally intended no ringing of wedding bells, only in the final sentence of the book, added at Bulwer-Lytton's insistence, giving promise of a happy end.

Consciousness of the nature of his reading public may also explain Dickens' portrayal of children. Where he is absolutely accurate and totally convincing is in the obviously autobiographical early chapters of both *Copperfield* and *Great Expectations*. But then the maudlin and the sentimental seem to take over. A topical Wordsworthian touch appears at times – the wonder of the child as Lizzie Hexham sees pictures in her fire or when Paul Dombey converses with the sea; and doubtless his middle-class readers would welcome the picture of a child like Little Nell being so solicitous to the comforts of her tiresome grandfather. There is perhaps a theatrical touch again in the way Dickens will hold his readers in intolerable suspense by choosing the moment when their sympathies are well and truly engaged to bring them almost to their knees by killing off their darling. The descriptions of the deaths of Little Nell, Paul Dombey and Jo the crossing-sweeper are shamelessly maudlin, but perhaps Dickens did not think so. After all, he cried over them himself.

In this tangled tale of fact interwoven with fiction, what survives in Dickens' novels of genuine value to the historian? In the first place, almost all Dickens' prejudices were shared by his readers, and this sheds valuable light on the contemporary attitudes of his social circle. G. M. Young once wrote that one of the two fundamental assumptions that remained inviolate through the whole of Victoria's reign was respect for 'the family as the primary social unit'. Dickens confirms this as his own sincere belief. 'Heaven's fallen sister, Home', he once wrote. Home meant snugness and security. Home was the essential setting of 'Happy Christmas one and all' (and the immense popularity of his regular Christmas stories provides another insight into Victorian values). Then again, he shared with his readers horror of anarchy and the potential violence of the mob, graphically described in both *Barnaby Rudge* and *The Tale of Two Cities*. For all his genuine sympathy for the poor, he believed in the maintenance of the existing class structure. Dickens had no love for Americans (he thought that the insertion of the American episode in *Chuzzlewit* would increase his sales), and, in harmony with his readers, no great love for the French either (it is interesting that his only female murderess was Madame Hortense in *Bleak House*).

Dickens was guilty at times of anachronisms, most especially in *Little Dorrit* and *Bleak House*. Nevertheless, the sequence of his novels provide a revealing guide to both significant and the more subtle changes that he witnessed during the course of his life. It was in 1822, when he was ten years old, that his family moved from Chatham to London. When he came to write *Barnaby Rudge* in 1841, he was able from memory to describe the great city as Gabriel Varden perceived it on a fateful journey there in 1780, because it had hardly changed by the 1820s—no railways, no urban sanitation, no restaurants but only taverns and chop houses and raw reminders of the fate of miscreants in the gaunt prisons, the pillory and public hangings. By the time he came to write *Our Mutual Friend*, the Inner Circle had been built and railways had thrust their way into the very heart of the City, slicing through Camden Town and causing Staggs Garden completely to disappear. It was the earlier London of his boyhood years that remained firmly rooted in Dickens' memory. But the changes that he observed are vividly recorded in his novels, especially the slum areas of Whitechapel, Shadwell and Wapping, which he was wont to call his 'Babylon'. He noted and described the genesis of suburbia, the jerry-building as one approached the Kent and Surrey borders. The houses 'looked like a toy neighbourhood taken in blocks out of a box by a child of particularly incoherent mind and set up anyhow'. It was 'as if the child had given the table a kick and gone to sleep'. For the fidelity of description of the changing face of London and how the railways (an enduring fascination for Dickens) had opened up and transformed the landscape, an historian could not hope to find a more graphic source.

The novels chart the progress of both a changing world and changing attitudes and priorities. The picaresque scenes of *The Pickwick Papers* and the London of the Veneerings and Rogue Riderhood belong to completely different periods of history. In *Dombey and Son*, poor Solomon Gills' trade in marine tackle, depleted into virtually nothing, stands as a pathetic survival. England has become more class-conscious, and money and speculation have become dominant themes. It has been observed that the evils that Dickens chooses to attack have changed too. In the early novels they were 'crime, hypocrisy, cruelty and the new Poor Law'. From *Bleak House* onwards, the new targets are Public Health and the neglect of sanitation. Dickens had never doubted that money was power (which is why he was so anxious to make more and more money for himself). It had the power to transform the lives of the less fortunate through benevolence; it had the power to ruin people, too. This becomes a central theme in the novels from *Dombey and Son* onwards. It is interesting that whereas Ralph Nickleby is depicted as an unscrupulous usurer, the fraudster Merdle in *Little Dorrit* appears rather as a helpless victim of the *Zeitgeist*, caught up in the speculative mania that has gripped the whole city.

For all Dickens' love of exaggeration and caricature, he often went to extraordinary lengths to achieve accuracy. He studied the vernacular of the prototypes of his characters, and liked to mimic them in order to make his dialogues authentic. The speech of Jo the crossing-sweeper was taken down verbatim from the cross-examination of one, George Ruby, at the Guildhall. He hired a Thames steamer in order to 'walk the course' of Magwitch's recapture in *Great Expectations*. He visited a taxidermist's shop near Seven Dials to find an authentic setting for Mr Venus, and he sought out an opium den for his observation before he wrote the opening scenes of *Edwin Drood*. But above all, there is one area, and a vast one, in which a historian must pay deference to the superior knowledge of Dickens. By nature, he was a *voyeur*; and what many people might have merely noted in passing, he perceived; and what he perceived he remembered with quite an extraordinary clarity. From whom else could one hope to find such a faithful picture of the interior of the Marshalsea, its smell, the deportment of its inmates? He knew, from experience and observation, exactly what was the procedure in an Insolvency Court. Having a morbid fascination for prisons, asylums and executions, he could give a more detailed account of a public hanging and the crowd's reaction to it than probably any official record. So intense was his curiosity in discovering precise details of grisly horrors that he attended a public guillotining in Rome, and insisted on viewing the result. To his astonishment he observed that when the head was severed from the body, the neck totally disappeared.

Dickens could recapture exactly the sort of curiosity, peculiar perhaps to an observant and imaginative child, whose vision tends to focus on the minutiæ of his surroundings, and most especially on specific features of adults he encounters. Not only did Dickens vividly recall these personal impressions of childhood, but he also retained the same way of regarding people and things when he grew up. David Copperfield was fascinated by the touch of Peggotty's forefinger, for instance, and 'its being roughened by needlework, like a pocket nutmeg grater'. When he regarded Mr Murdstone at close quarters, he noticed that 'his hair and whiskers were blacker and thicker, looked at so near, than ever I had given them credit for being. A squareness about the lower part of his face, and the dotted indication of the strong black beard he shaved close every day, reminded me of a waxwork that had travelled into our neighbourhood some half a year before'.

John Carey, commenting on this unique feature of Dickens' imaginative art, suggests that he always tended to regard other people, and hence his fictional characters, 'in fragments'. So the anatomical motif he chooses for the dominant feature of the bad Mr Carker in *Dombey* is his 'teeth', which sometimes 'bristle' and sometimes 'glow', but always identify his feelings and his motives. Captain Bunsby, in the same book, to whom Ned Cuttle always defers on matter of seamanship, has a singular eye, because it roves in such a way that it never focuses on the person he is addressing. Inspector Bucket has a significant fat finger ‘which he shakes threateningly at suspects and presses to his ear as if it were whispering information’. At some time or other, Dickens would have observed idiosyncrasies of this sort in actual people, and then treasured them in his memory for later use.

All of which is to say that Dickens’ writings contain hundreds of miniature vignettes of the times in which he lived which would probably never have occurred to any other chronicler to record: the freemasonry among London cab-drivers, for instance, who saluted each other by ‘the solemn lifting of the little finger of the right hand’; or the spectacle which surprised Dickens as a youth when he came across a group of London coal-heavers dancing outside a tavern near Scotland Yard.

These are little things; but they are also precious evocations of the real flesh and blood of an age long past; and perhaps it is these little things which succeed in making the past live again for us. I am indebted to Peter Ackroyd for perceiving the significance of a remark which Dickens puts into the mouth of David Copperfield, when in looking back over his experiences, he comes to the conclusion that ‘trifles are the sum of life’. They are surely the very stuff of history, too.

REFERENCES

David Newsome did not feel that it was necessary to include references for all the essays in this book, since they are aimed at a general readership. The references for four of these essays are the footnotes compiled for their original publication, with minor editorial alterations.

IV THOMAS ARNOLD: A BICENTENARY APPRAISAL

1. A. J. P. Stanley, *The Life and Correspondence of Thomas Arnold*, 2 vols (London: Fellowes, 8th edition, 1858), vol.II, p.282.
2. A. O. J. Cockshut, *Truth to Life. The Art of Biography in the Nineteenth Century* (London: Collins, 1974), p.88.
3. Stanley, *Arnold*, vol.1, p.153.
4. Lytton Strachey, *Eminent Victorians* (London: Chatto & Windus, 1948), p.205.
5. C. S. Dessain, *John Henry Newman* (London: Nelson, 1966), p.44; D. C. Lathbury, *Correspondence on Church and Religion of W.E. Gladstone*, 2 vols (London: John Murray, 1910), vol.1, p.485.
6. Amy Cruse, *The Victorians and their Books* (London: Allen & Unwin, 1935), p.117.
7. R. E. Prothero & G. G. Bradley, *The Life and Correspondence of Arthur Penrhyn Stanley*, 2 vols (London: John Murray, 1893), vol.1, p.319.
8. Humphry House, *The Dickens World* (Oxford University Press, 1942), p.93.
9. Stanley, *Arnold*, vol.2, p.137.
10. E. C. Mack, *Public Schools and British Opinion, 1780-1860* (London: Methuen, 1938), p.331.
11. Stanley, *Arnold*, vol.1, p.67.
12. *Ibid.*, p.209.
13. *Ibid.*, p.27.
14. *Ibid.*, vol.2, p.40.
15. *Ibid.*, vol.1, p.33.
16. In Walter E. Houghton, *The Victorian Frame of Mind 1830-1870* (New Haven and London: Yale University Press, 1957), p.221.

17. Norman Vance, *The Sinews of the Spirit: The Ideal of Christian Manliness in Victorian Literature and Thought* (Cambridge University Press, 1985), p.71.
18. *Ibid.*, p.24.
19. G. M. Young, *Portrait of an Age: Victorian England*, annotated by G. Kitson Clark (Oxford University Press, 1977), p.213.
20. Stanley, *Arnold*, vol.1, pp.34-5.
21. Charles Dickens, *Pickwick Papers*, Chapter XXVIII.
22. J. F. C. Harrison, *A History of the Working Men's College 1854-1954* (London: Routledge & Kegan Paul, 1954), p.38.
23. David Newsome, *A History of Wellington College, 1859-1959* (London: John Murray, 1959), p.101.
24. A. C. Benson, *The Leaves of the Tree. Studies in Biography* (New York and London: Smith, Elder & Co., 1911), p.61.
25. Stanley, *Arnold*, vol.1, p.44.
26. Michael McCrum, *Thomas Arnold, Headmaster. A Reassessment* (Oxford University Press, 1989), p.116.
27. Stanley, *Arnold*, vol.2, pp.36-7.
28. T. W. Bamford, *Thomas Arnold* (London: Cresset Press, 1960), *passim*.
29. A. J. H. Reeve, 'Aspects of the Life of Dr Thomas Arnold (1795-1842) in the light of the unpublished correspondence', University of Hull PhD thesis, 1988, pp.262-4.
30. *Ibid.*, pp.356-9.
31. R. M. Ogilvie, *Latin and Greek. A History of the Influence of the Classics on English Life from 1600-1918* (London: Routledge, 1964), p.98.
32. *Ibid.*, p.102.
33. A. P. Stanley (ed.), *Miscellaneous Works of Thomas Arnold* (London: Fellowes, 1858), p.399.
34. Young, *Victorian England*, p.105.
35. Harold Perkin, *The Origins of Modern English Society, 1780-1880* (London: Routledge & Kegan Paul, 1969), p.298.
36. Alexis de Tocqueville, *Journeys in England and Ireland*, ed. J.p.Mayer (London: Faber & Faber, 1958), pp.55-6.
37. Gertrude Himmelfarb, *Victorian Minds* (London: Weidenfeld & Nicolson, 1968), p.277.
38. Stanley, *Arnold*, vol.1, p.158.
39. Vance, *Sinews of the Spirit*, p.70.
40. Boyd Hilton, *The Age of Atonement. The Influence of Evangelicalism on Social and Economic Thought, 1795-1865* (Oxford University Press, 1988), p.131.

41. Stanley, *Arnold*, vol.1, p.264.
42. *Ibid.*, vol.2, p.160.
43. Thomas Arnold, *Introductory Lectures on Modern History* (London: Longmans, Green & Co., 1874), pp.30-1.
44. Thomas Arnold, *Principles of Church Reform*, ed. M. J. Jackson & J. Rogan (London: SPCK, 1962), p.66.
45. Stanley, *Arnold*, vol.1, p.187.
46. *Ibid.*, vol.2, pp.49-50.
47. *Ibid.*, vol.1, p.178.
48. *Ibid.*, vol.1, p.38.
49. *Ibid.*, vol.2, p.204.
50. *Ibid.*, vol.1, p.310.
51. *Ibid.*, vol.2, pp.245-6.
52. Duncan Forbes, *The Liberal Anglican Idea of History* (Cambridge University Press, 1952).
53. Stanley, *Arnold*, vol.2, p.242.
54. Prothero, *Stanley*, vol.1, p.362.
55. Forbes, *Anglican Idea*, p.16.
56. *Ibid.*, p.93.
57. Stanley, *Arnold*, vol.1, p.223.
58. *Ibid.*, vol.1, p.164.
59. Fanny Kingsley (ed.), *Charles Kingsley. Letters and Memories of his Life* (London: Kegan Paul, 1877), vol.1, p.88.
60. Stanley, *Arnold*, vol.1, p.166.
61. D. G. James, *Matthew Arnold and the Decline of English Romanticism* (Oxford: Clarendon Press, 1961), p.2.
62. G.W.E. Russell (ed.), *Letters of Matthew Arnold, 1848-1888*, (London: Macmillan, 1895), vol.1, p.391.
63. E. Abbott & L. Campbell, *The Life and Letters of Benjamin Jowett*, 2 vols (London: John Murray, 1897), vol.2, p.161.

V NEWMAN AND THE OXFORD MOVEMENT

1. MS. letter from Robert Carr to R. I. Wilberforce, quoted in my *The Parting of Friends* (1966), p.15.
2. A. Mozley (ed.), *Letters and Correspondence of John Henry Newman* (1891), Letter 204.
3. M. Pattison, *Memoirs* (1885), p.236.
4. R. W. Church, *The Oxford Movement, Twelve Years 1833-1845* (1891), pp.139-41.

5. T. Mozley, *Reminiscences chiefly of Oriel College and the Oxford Movement* (1882), I, p.313.
6. These were the Bampton Lectures of 1832, entitled Sscholastic Philosophy considered in its relation to Christian Theology'. See H. P. Liddon, *Life of E. B. Pusey* (1854), I, pp.361-4.
7. J. H. Newman, *Apologia pro vita sua.* Wilfred Ward's edition (1913), p.7.
8. This was Thomas Arnold. See my *The Parting of Friends,* p. 165.
9. William Palmer, *A Narrative of Events connected with the Publication of the Tracts for the Times* (1883), p.99.
10. Y. Brilioth, *Evangelicalism and the Oxford Movement: Three Lectures* (1934), p.28.
11. See my *The Parting of Friends,* p.316.
12. J. H. Newman, *Apologia,* p.119.
13. J. A. Froude, *Short Studies on Great Subjects* (1891), IV, pp.278-80.
14. J. B. Mozley, *Lectures and other Theological Papers* (1883), p.281.
15. See the argument, full of self-revelatory detail, in J. H. Newman, *A Grammar of Assent* (1906 edition), pp.415-18.
16. *Apologia,* p.150.
17. *Ibid.* p.118.
18. From a MS letter of John Sargent to Samuel Wilberforce; see my *The Parting of Friends*, p.85.
19. Christopher Dawson, *The Spirit of the Oxford Movement* (1945), p.16.
20. Sir G. Prevost (ed.), *The Autobiography of Isaac Williams* (2nd edn, 1892), p.118, note 1.
21. MS letter of John Keble to R. I. Wilberforce, quoted in *The Parting of Friends* (1966), p.394.
22. R. W. Church, *Occasional Papers* (1897), II, pp.472-3.
23. J. H. Newman, *Grammar of Assent,* Note II, p.499.
24. J. H. Newman, *Apologia*, pp.119-29.
25. J. H. Newman, *Callista* (1855); Nicholas Wiseman, *Fabiola* (1854); R. I. Wilberforce, *Rutilius and Lucius* (1842).
26. Newman in a letter to G. D. Ryder, see *The Parting of Friends*, p.153.
27. J. H. Newman, *The Arians of the Fourth Century: their Doctrine, Temper and Conduct* (1833).
28. J. H. Newman, *Historical Sketches* (1872), II, p.342.
29. See especially Owen Chadwick, *From Bossuet to Newman. The Idea of Doctrinal Development* (Cambridge, 1957), pp.143-4.
30. J. H. Newman, *Sermons bearing on Subjects of the Day* (1918 edn), p.390.
31. J. H. Newman, *Arians* , p.47.

32. Isaac Williams, 'On Reserve in Communicating Religious Knowledge', Part I, *Tract 80* (1835) in *Tracts for the Times* IV, p.61.
33. J. H. Newman, *Arians*, pp.55-6.
34. Thomas Arnold, 'Essay on the Right Interpretation and Understanding of the Scriptures' in *Sermons,* II (1878 edn), pp.286-7.
35. See my article 'Justification and Sanctification: Newman and the Evangelicals' in *Journal of Theological Studies* NS Vol. XV, Part I (1964), pp.49-50.
36. See Walter Lock, *John Keble* (1893), p.48.
37. John Keble, *Occasional Papers and Reviews* (1877), pp.102-3.
38. J. H. Newman, *Sermons on Subjects of the Day,* pp.140-1.
39. E. S. Purcell, *Life of Cardinal Manning* (1896), I, p.233.
40. J. H. Newman, *Sermons on Subjects of the Day,* p.391.
41. R. W. Church, *Occasional Papers,* II, p.473.
42. *Letters and Diaries of John Henry Newman,* ed. C. S. Dessain, XIII (1963), pp.295-6.
43. J. H. Newman, *Apologia,* p.132.

VII HOW SOAPY WAS SAM?

1. R. W. Church, *Occasional Papers* (London 1897), II. p.336.
2. William Palmer, *A Narrative of Events connected with the Publication of the Tracts for the Times* (London 1883), p.256; see also J. W. Burgon, *Lives of Twelve Good Men* (London 1888), II, pp.1-70, J. H. Overton and E. Wordsworth, *Christopher Wordsworth, Bishop of Lincoln* (London: 1890), pp.117-8.
3. Y. Brilioth, *Three Lectures on Evangelicalism and the Oxford Movement* (London 1934), p.38; see also R. K. Pugh's unpublished Oxford DPhil thesis 'The Episcopate of Samuel Wilberforce' (1957), pp.10 & 416, and Christopher Dawson, *The Spirit of the Oxford Movement* (London 1945), p.113.
4. *The Spectator,* 23 December 1882, referring to a letter of R. G. Wilberforce in *The Times*, 22 December 1882. See also *Pall Mall Gazette,* 23 December 1882, article entitled 'Editorial Discretion'.
5. G. C. B. Davies, *Henry Phillpotts, Bishop of Exeter* (London 1954), p.210.
6. A. R. Ashwell, *Life of Samuel Wilberforce* (London 1880), I, p.486.
7. *The Greville Memoirs*, second part (London 1885), III, pp.114-8. Compare Greville's earlier opinion of Samuel in II, pp.264, 410-12.

8. T. Mozley, *Reminiscences chiefly of Oriel College and the Oxford Movement* (London 1882), I, p.104.
9. Wrangham MSS., S.W. Box 1, no.152.
10. Sandwith MSS., B.I. no. 19, letter of Henry Wilberforce to R. I. Wilberforce, 29 May 1883.
11. Wrangham MSS., S.W. Box 2, no.213.
12. *Ibid.,* Box 1, no.177.
13. Wrangham MSS., S.W. Box 1, no.183.
14. *Ibid.*, Box i, no.202.
15. A. R. Ashwell, *op.cit.,* I, p.173.
16. Wrangham MSS., S.W. Box 2, no.231; Ashwell, *op.cit.*, I, p.206. See also Wrangham MSS., Box 2, no.241: 'I have seen a good deal of Croker lately'.
17. W. J. Jennings (editor), *The Correspondence and Diaries of John Wilson Croker* (London 1884), II, pp.410-11, and III, pp.2-3.
18. *Ibid.,* III, pp.2-3.
19. R. K. Pugh, 'The Episcopate of Samuel Wilberforce', p.15. I am indebted to Dr Pugh for permission to quote this passage. The original letters are in the British Museum Add. MSS. 40575. fol.331-2 and fol.408.
20. Wrangham MSS., S.W. Box 2, no.270.
21. Ibid., Box 2, no.283.
22. Henfield MSS., Letters of Gladstone to S. Wilberforce, no.168.
23. Wrangham MSS., S.W. Box, no.285.

VIII THE ASSAULT ON MAMMON

1. J. N. Figgis, *Antichrist, and other Sermons,* London 1913, i.
2. George Dangerfield, *The Strange Death of Liberal England 1910-1914,* Capricorn edition, 1961.
3. J. N. Figgis, *op.cit.,* p.31.
4. By Lothar of Segni, the future pope Innocent III, a lugubrious treatise in three books (P[atrologia]. L[atina]., ccxvii, col.701ff.), which enjoyed considerable popularity in the thirteenth and fourteenth centuries.
5. W. L. Burn, *The Age of Equipoise: a Study of the Mid-Victorian Generation,* London 1964, p.65.
6. Thomas Carlyle, *Past and Present,* Everyman edition, 1941, pp.140-1.
7. Quoted in C. F. G. Masterman, *The Condition of England,* London 1909, and in J. N. Figgis, *Civilisation at the Cross Roads,* London 1913, p.100.

8. J. E. C. Bodley, 'The Decay of Idealism in France', in *Cardinal Manning, and other Essays,* London 1912, p.142.
9. *Ibid.,* p.108.
10. *Ibid.,* p.162.
11. J. P. T. Bury, *France 1814-1940,* London 1949, p.188.
12. Quoted by Roger Lloyd, *The Church of England in the Twentieth Century,* London 1946, i, p.39.
13. G. B. Shaw, *Major Barbara,* Penguin edition, 1945, p.87.
14. V. Sackville-West, *The Edwardians,* London: 1930.
15. R. Lloyd, *op.cit.,* p.41.
16. G. K. Chesterton, *Orthodoxy,* London 1909, p.44.
17. R. Lloyd, *op.cit.,* p.40.
18. G. L. Prestige, *The Life of Charles Gore,* London 1935, p.225.
19. J. N. Figgis, *Civilisation at the Cross Roads,* pp.74-5.
20. D. G. Nicholls, 'Authority in Church and State. Aspects of the Thought of J. N. Figgis and his contemporaries' (unpublished PhD thesis, 1962, deposited in the Cambridge University Library), p.31.
21. See G. K. A. Bell, *Randall Davidson, Archbishop of Canterbury* (third edition, 1952), pp.474-80; J. N. Figgis, *Civilisation at the Cross Roads,* pp.78-80.
22. G. L. Prestige, *op.cit.,* p.159. See also Charles Gore, *The New Theology and the Old Religion,* London 1907, pp.291-2. 'We must dissociate the clergy from being identified with the wealthier classes'.
23. Charles Gore, *The Social Doctrine of the Sermon on the Mount,* Oxford 1904, p.13.
24. James Carpenter, *Gore: a Study in Liberal Catholic Thought,* London: 1960, p.250.
25. J. N. Figgis, *Some Defects in English Religion, and other Sermons,* London 1917, pp.19-28.
26. J. N. Figgis, *Churches in the Modern State,* London 1913, p.51-2.
27. K. S. Inglis, *Churches and the Working Classes in Victorian England,* London 1963, p.280.
28. Stephen Paget, *Henry Scott Holland, Memoir and Letters,* London 1921, p.241.
29. J. N. Figgis, *Civilisation at the Cross Roads,* ix.
30. Charles Gore, *The Incarnation of the Son of God,* Bampton Lectures for 1891, London 1896, pp.210-11.
31 James Carpenter, *op.cit.,* pp.248-9.
32. Melvin Richter, *The Politics of Conscience: T. H. Green and his Age,* London 1964, pp.126-7.
33. D. G. Nicholls, *op.cit.,* p.295.

34. J. N. Figgis, *Churches in the Modern State,* p.47.
35. G. L. Prestige, *op.cit.,* p.14.
36. J. N. Figgis, *Churches in the Modern State,* Appendix II, p.229.
37. J. N. Figgis, *Civilisation at the Cross Roads,* p.53.
38. J. N. Figgis, *The Gospel and Human Needs,* London 1909, p.150.
39. J. N. Figgis, *Churches in the Modern State,* p.249. Gierke's book the *Deutsche Genossenschaftrecht,* Maitland 'once declared to me to be the greatest book he had ever read'.
40. *Ibid.,* p.250.
41. William McDougal, *The Group Mind,* Cambridge 1920, p.19. McDougal discusses the influence of Maitland in transmitting the ideas of Gierke.
42. J. N. Figgis, *Civilisation at the Cross Roads,* p.23.
43. *Ibid.,* p.78.
44. Charles Gore, *The Incarnation of the Son of God,* p.187.
45. Charles Gore, *The Social Doctrine of the Sermon on the Mount,* p.17.
46. J. H. Newman, *Sermons bearing on Subjects of the Day,* London 1918, pp.390, 393.
47. G. L. Prestige, *op.cit.,* pp.9-10; J. Carpenter, *op.cit.,* pp.25-6.
48. B. F. Westcott, *Disciplined Life: three Addresses,* London 1886, p.13.
49. Charles Gore, *Buying up the Opportunity,* London 1895, pp.13 & 15.
50. A. Westcott, *The Life and Letters of Brooke Foss Westcott,* London 1903, i, pp.264-5.
51. A. C. Benson, *The Life of Edward White Benson,* London 1899, i, pp.260-1; A. F. Hort, *The Life and Letters of Fenton John Anthony Hort,* London 1896, ii, pp.103-5.
52. Charles Gore, *The Social Doctrine of the Sermon on the Mount,* p.18.
53. A. Westcott, *op.cit.,* i, p.264.
54. B. F. Westcott, *Essays in the History of Religious Thought in the West,* London 1891.
55. J. N. Figgis, *Civilisation at the Cross Roads,* pp.76-8.
56. Charles Gore, *Buying up the Opportunity,* pp.10-13.

www.ingramcontent.com/pod-product-compliance
Ingram Content Group UK Ltd.
Pitfield, Milton Keynes, MK11 3LW, UK
UKHW021051270726
13967UKWH00012B/568